Dream Notes

THEODOR W. ADORNO

Dream Notes

Edited by CHRISTOPH GÖDDE and HENRI LONITZ

Afterword by JAN PHILIPP REEMTSMA

Translated by
RODNEY LIVINGSTONE

polity

First published in German as Traumprotokolle,
© Suhrkamp Verlag Franfurt am Main 2005
English edition © Polity Press, 2007

This paperback edition © Polity Press, 2020

Polity Press
65 Bridge Street
Cambridge CB2 1UR, UK

Polity Press
101 Station Landing
Suite 300
Medford, MA 02155, USA

ISBN-10: 0-7456-3830-9
ISBN-13: 978-0-7456-3830-0
ISBN-10: 0-7456-3831-7 (pb)
ISBN-13: 978-0-7456-3831-7 (pb)

A catalogue record for this book is available from the British Library.

Typeset in 10.5/15pt Fournier by Servis Filmsetting Limited, Stockport, Cheshire

Printed and bound by TJ International

The publisher has used its best endeavours to ensure that the URLs for external websites referred to in this book are correct and active at the time of going to press. However, the publisher has no responsibility for the websites and can make no guarantee that a site will remain live or that the content is or will remain appropriate.

Every effort has been made to trace all copyright holders, but if any have been overlooked the publisher will be pleased to include any necessary credits in any subsequent reprint or edition.

For further information on Polity, visit our website:
politybooks.com

— Contents —

— Editorial Foreword —

Early in January 1956, Adorno noted down two ideas about dreams that testify to his particular interest in a central theory of dreams and the interconnectedness of his own dreams. 'Certain dream experiences lead me to believe that the individual experiences his own death as a cosmic catastrophe.' And, 'Our dreams are linked with each other not just because they are "ours", but because they form a continuum, they belong to a unified world, just as, for example, all Kafka's stories inhabit "the same world". The more dreams hang together or are repeated, the greater the danger that we shall be unable to distinguish between them and reality.' This second reflection was followed by the dream that he wrote down from memory on 9 January 1956. The idea that dreams are connected by certain motifs is what induced him to select a number of them for publication. This selection did not appear while Adorno was still alive, but Rolf Tiedemann included it in Volume 20 of the *Gesammelte Schriften*. It is based on a typescript preceded by Adorno's own preliminary comment: 'These Dream Notes, which have been chosen from a much larger collection, are authentic. I wrote them all down immediately on waking and in preparing them for publication have only corrected the most obvious linguistic lapses.' 'A much larger collection' refers not just to the great number of dreams recorded in the notebooks, but also to a bundle of papers that were then copied by Gretel Adorno with diplomatic accuracy. The present volume adds to the dream notes already published by drawing on the copies existing in typescript. A comparison between the copies and original typescripts confirms that Adorno's alterations were largely confined to correcting the linguistic mistakes that arose from the haste with which he recorded the dreams and also from changing the names of people either to their initials or to periphrases such as 'my friend' or 'my doctor'. For example, he replaced Rudolf Kolisch's nickname 'Rudi' with his surname. On the other hand, he retained the names where he believed the content was harmless. Apart from obvious typing mistakes, Gretel Adorno's copies were not further edited and have been reproduced in full. A few errors in transcription have been corrected, as have the dates of the dreams given in the *Gesammelte Schriften* as 1 February 1942 and 22 May 1942 [which have now been changed to January 1942 and 22 May 1941 respectively]. A few names were made anonymous in the copies; in one case Eduard was replaced by his surname Steuermann. The notes to the dreams have been added by the translator. The notes to the Afterword are by Jan Philipp Reemtsma except where indicated.

Dreams are as black as death.
THEODOR W. ADORNO

— *Dream Notes* —

Frankfurt, January 1934

In my dream, I was travelling with G. in a large, very comfortable bus down from Pontresina to the Lower Engadine. The bus was quite full and there was no lack of people I knew: the much travelled illustrator Miss P. and an old professor in industry and his wife were among them. However, the bus did not travel along the Engadine road, but went somewhere near my home town: between Königstein and Kronberg.[1] On a large bend the bus went too far onto the right side of the road and one of its front wheels became suspended over a ditch for what seemed to me to be a very long time. 'I have seen this happen before', said the much travelled illustrator in the tone of someone who knew what she was talking about. 'The bus will go on like this for a bit and will then turn over and we shall all be dead.' That same moment the bus plunged over the side. Suddenly, I came to and found myself standing up, facing G.; both of us were unharmed. I realized I was crying as I said, 'I would so like to have kept on being alive with you.' Only then did I notice that my body was completely smashed up. At the moment of death, I awoke.

---

[1] These are small, rather exclusive towns in the Taunus hills to the north of Frankfurt.

Oxford, 9 June 1936

Dream: Agathe[2] appeared to me and said in a sorrowful voice: 'My child, I always used to say to you that we shall meet again after our death. Today, I can only tell you: I don't know. –'

Oxford, 10 March 1937

I found myself in Paris without any money, but wanted to visit a particularly elegant brothel, the Maison Drouot (in reality, Hôtel Drouot is the best-known auction house for antiques). I asked Friedel to lend me some money: 200 francs. To my great astonishment he gave them to me, saying, however: 'I only give them you because the food in the Hôtel Drouot is so outstanding.' In fact, without even catching a glimpse of a girl, I did eat in the bar – a beefsteak that made me so happy that I forgot about everything else. It was served with a white sauce.

In another dream, earlier the same night, I saw Agathe. She said: 'My child, you mustn't be cross with me, but if I owned two genuine valleys, I would give up all of Schubert's music in exchange.'

London, 1937
(while he was working on *In Search of Wagner*)

My dream had a title: 'Siegfried's last adventure' or 'Siegfried's last death'. It took place on a vast stage which

---

[2] Agathe was Adorno's aunt. She had lived with the family ever since his parents' marriage and was a major influence on him both when he was a child and later on.

did not just represent a landscape but actually was one: small rocks and a lot of vegetation, rather like in the mountains leading up to the Alpine pastures. Siegfried was striding through this theatrical landscape toward the rear, accompanied by someone, I cannot remember who. He was dressed half in mythological, half in modern clothes, a little bit like for a rehearsal. Finally, he discovered his adversary, a figure in riding dress: grey-green linen suit, riding breeches and brown riding boots. He started to fight with him, but their struggle was plainly all in fun. It mainly consisted of his wrestling with his opponent, who was already on the ground and who seemed happy to let this happen. Siegfried soon succeeded in forcing him onto his back until his shoulders touched the ground, and he was either declared the loser or he admitted as much. Unexpectedly, however, Siegfried drew a small dagger from his jacket pocket, where he kept it on a small clip, as if it were a fountain pen. He hurled the knife at his opponent's chest from close to, as if in play. The latter groaned aloud and it became clear that it was a woman. She quickly made her escape, saying that she would now have to die alone in her little house, that was the hardest thing of all. She disappeared into a building that looked like the ones belonging to the Darmstadt artist colony. Siegfried sent his companion after her with instructions to take possession of her treasures. Brünnhilde then appeared in the background in the shape of the Statue of Liberty in New York. Sounding like a nagging wife, she screamed, 'I want a ring, I want a beautiful ring, don't forget to take her ring from her.' This was how Siegfried obtained the ring of the Nibelung.

New York, November or December 1938

I dreamt that Hölderlin was called Hölderlin because he was always playing a flute made of elder wood [*Holunder*].

New York, 30 December 1940

Just before waking up, I witnessed the scene illustrated by Baudelaire's poem *Don Juan aux enfers*, probably taken from a picture by Delacroix. However, instead of stygian night it was broad daylight and an American public festival by the waterside. There stood a large white sign – belonging to a steamer station – with a garish red inscription saying 'ALABAMT'. Don Juan's barque had a long, narrow funnel – a ferry boat ('Ferry Boat Serenade'). Unlike in Baudelaire, the hero does not stand in silence. In his Spanish costume – black and violet – he speaks incessantly and vociferously, like a salesman. My thought was: an out-of-work actor. But not content with vehement statements and gestures, he began mercilessly to thrash Charon – a figure who remained undefined. He then announced that he was an American and that he wouldn't stand for all this. He wouldn't let himself be shut up in a box. This statement was greeted with a wave of applause, as if he were a champion. He then strode past the onlookers, who were cordoned off from him. I shuddered and found the entire scene ridiculous, but my main worry was that the crowd would take a dislike to us. When he came to where we were, A. complimented him on his talented performance. I have forgotten his reply, but his tone was anything but friendly. After that, we started to ask questions about the fate of the characters in *Carmen* in the next world. 'Is Micaela looking good?' 'Awful', replied Don Juan in a rage. 'But surely Carmen is all right', I insisted. 'No', he said, but it seemed to me that his anger was fading. At that point, the boats on the Hudson tooted that it was 8 a.m. and I woke up.

New York, 8 February 1941

I was on a ship that had been boarded by pirates. They clambered up the sides, there were even some women among them. But my wish that they should be overpowered prevailed. At any rate, in the next scene their fate was decided. They all had to die; to be shot and their bodies thrown overboard. I objected, but not from any feelings of humanity. It would be a pity, I said, that the women should be killed without our having taken our pleasure with them. Everyone agreed with me. I went down into the space where the pirates were being held – the low-ceilinged lounge of a medium-sized steamer. The pirates all sat in prehistoric silence. The men, heavily shackled, were dressed in old-fashioned clothing. Loaded pistols lay on the table in front of them. The brides were around five in number, dressed in modern clothes. I have a distinct memory of two of them. One was German. She fitted exactly my image of a tart – in a red dress, her hair peroxide blond like a bar-girl, on the plump side, but very attractive; her profile made her look a little sheep-like. The other girl was a delightful young mulatto, dressed quite simply in a brown knitted woollen dress, the kind of woman one sees in Harlem. The women went into a side room and I told them to undress. They obeyed, that is, the tart started to take her clothes off right away. The mulatto girl refused to do so. 'This is the style of the Institute', she said, 'not the Circus style.'[3] When I asked what she meant, she explained that in the circus world, to which she belonged, a body was such an everyday matter that no one took any interest in nakedness. Things were different, she thought, in my world. This is why my sister (= L.) let no opportunity slip to show off as much of herself as possible.

Los Angeles, 22 May 1941

We were walking, my mother, Agathe and I, on a ridge path of a reddish sandstone hue familiar to me from Amorbach. But we were on the West Coast of America. Far below, to the left, lay the Pacific Ocean. At one point the footpath seemed to become steeper or to peter out altogether. I set about looking for a better path off to the right, through rocks and undergrowth. After a few steps I came to a large plateau. I thought I had now found the way. But I soon discovered that the vegetation concealed the dizziest precipices in every direction, and that there was no way to reach the plain that stretched inland and that I had mistakenly thought to be part of the plateau. There, at frighteningly regular intervals, I saw groups of people with apparatuses, surveyors perhaps. I looked for the way back to the first path, and found it too. When I rejoined my mother and Agathe a laughing black couple suddenly stood in our path; he was dressed in bold checked trousers, she in a grey sporting costume. We walked on. Soon we met

[3] This sentence was in English in the original.

a black child. 'We must be close to a settlement', I said. There were a number of huts or caves made of sand or cut into the hillside. A gateway passed through one of them. We went through and stood, overwhelmed with joy, on the square in front of the palace of Bamberg – the 'Schnatterloch' in Miltenberg.[4]

Los Angeles, 20 November 1941

In my first night in Los Angeles I dreamt I had arranged to meet a girl of the loosest morals in a café – in Paris? She kept me waiting. Finally, I was called to a phone booth. I shouted into the phone, 'Are you coming at long last?', and also something intimate. From a long way off I heard a voice reply, 'This is Professor MacIver'. He wanted to tell me something of importance concerning the courses at the institute. He also said something about a 'misunderstanding'. He went on speaking, but I did not understand what he said, partly because I was still thinking about the girl and partly because his voice was too muffled.

Los Angeles, January 1942

On the Untermain Quay in Frankfurt I was caught up in the march-past of an Arab army. I asked King Ali Faisal to let me through and he agreed. I entered a beautiful house.

[4] In his childhood, Adorno's family often spent their holidays in Amorbach, a small town in the forested region of the Odenwald, south-east of Frankfurt. The walk from Amorbach to the neighbouring town of Miltenberg ended in a gate which the children called the Schnatterloch = 'Chatterhole', because it was often so cold it made their teeth chatter.

After some unclear happenings I was shown onto another floor, leading to President Roosevelt, who had his small private office there. He received me with great warmth. However, just in the way one speaks to children, he told me that I didn't have to pay attention the whole time, but could go ahead and read a book. All sorts of people came to visit without my taking any notice. Finally, a tall, sun-bronzed man appeared to whom Roosevelt introduced me. It was Knudsen.[5] The president said that he had some defence matters to discuss and he would have to ask me to leave the room. But I should definitely come to visit him again. He scribbled down his name, address and telephone number on a scrap of paper that had already been written on. – The lift didn't take me back to the ground floor and the exit, but down into the basement. There I found myself in the greatest danger. If I stayed in the lift shaft, I would be crushed to death; if I tried to climb out to the space surrounding it – I was scarcely tall enough for that – I would become entangled in the cables and ropes. Someone told me that I should try to climb up to some higher ground, heaven knows where. I said something about crocodiles, but took the advice. The crocodiles were already coming closer; their heads were those of extraordinarily beautiful women. One spoke kindly to me, saying that being eaten didn't hurt. To

[5] William Knudsen (1879–1948) was an executive in the automobile industry, working for both Ford and General Motors, where he served as president from 1937 to 1940. In 1940 President Roosevelt invited him to Washington to help with war production. Promoted to the rank of general, he worked as a consultant at the War Department until 1945.

help convince me she promised me the loveliest things beforehand.

A few nights later

I went with my mother to hear a performance of *The Mastersingers*. The entire dream took place during the performance, although the shadowy events on the stage had no connection with Wagner's plot. Only at one point did I seem to recognize Act Two. We were sitting in the front of one of the large balcony boxes over the stage. At the back of the box there was a large party of people who I realized were Frankfurt patricians. They began to make a huge row which was directed at a tall, good-looking man with a manly chest who was wearing tails and who was standing in the stalls next to one of the stalls boxes. I felt it was my duty to join in the row and shouted some highly insulting remarks at him. He instantly singled me out from among his enemies and shouted that I should come down and face him if I dared. I answered that it was beneath me to fight a con-man like him, but it did not sound very convincing. The patricians rushed down the stairs from the boxes and fell upon him. In the meantime, the mood of the glitteringly dressed audience began to turn against me and, with my mother's agreement, I thought it advisable to leave the box for a while. Long gap. Then, I was back in the box, but hidden. Act Two. On leaving the theatre with other people I knew, I encountered a wealthy, self-important girl. She remonstrated with me about the man in tails. 'But surely you know him. He is X the bank director.'

Los Angeles, end of May 1942

I dreamt I was to be crucified. The crucifixion was to take place at the Bockenheimer Warte, just by the university.[6] I felt no fear throughout the entire process. Bockenheim resembled a village on Sunday, deathly quiet, as if under glass. I observed it closely on my way to the place of execution. I imagined that the appearance of things on this my last day would enable me to glean some definite knowledge of the next world. At the same time, however, I declared that one should beware of arriving at premature conclusions. One should not let oneself be seduced into ascribing objective truth to the religion practised there simply because Bockenheim was still at the stage of simple commodity production. That aside, I was worried about whether I would obtain leave from the crucifixion to attend a large, extremely elegant dinner to which I had been invited, though I was confidently looking forward to it.

Los Angeles, early July 1942

The dream was – or seemed to me in retrospect – one long, unusually complicated detective story in which I was personally involved. I have forgotten what it was about. I only remember the end. I was with Agathe, who was in possession of the three most important pieces of evidence in the case. These were a clasp, a diamond ring and a cheap little reproduction – perhaps a medallion – of a well-known picture (by Gainsborough or Reynolds?) portraying a

---

[6] The Bockenheimer Warte, a surviving medieval fortified tower, is a well-known landmark near Frankfurt University.

small child dressed in light blue and with a white wig. It may have had something to do with soap bubbles. I felt reassured by the sight of these three pieces of evidence: they would prove my innocence at the trial. I then looked more closely at the picture of the child and realized to my inexpressible horror that it was a picture of me as a child. This was proof of my guilt, which consisted in the fact that I was that child – or simply a child? I wasted no time with denials but said at once to Agathe that only two possibilities remained: either immediate flight and concealment, or suicide. She said very firmly that only the latter came into consideration. Overcome by fear and horror, I awoke.

Los Angeles, 13 September 1942

We had been invited for the afternoon to celebrate Schoenberg's sixty-eighth birthday. Beforehand, around 2 p.m., I lay down and fell into a deep sleep until around 4. I woke up with a dream. Someone rang the bell here in our house in Brentwood. I was wearing sunglasses, but – unlike in real life – they prevented me from seeing properly. So I opened the door without being able to see who it was. It was an extraordinarily tall man. I scarcely came up to his waist: he was a giant, in fact, but this term did not actually occur to me. I just thought: what a tall man. He had a thick, bushy, greyish blond moustache. Then I realized that it was Wald, the coachman from Amorbach (such a person really exists, he had a house on the Gotthard and I once mistook him for B. H., a well-off friend of my father's, a mistake which for a long time I blamed myself for, thinking of it as one of the most tactless episodes of my entire life). So I addressed him as Herr Wald and, in his rumbustious, slightly menacing manner, he seemed excited to see me. 'Didn't you end up taking over the house belonging to Herr Bayer (his wealthy Amorbach boss)?' – 'Yes.' – 'And what brings you to Los Angeles?' – Well, that's a long story. It all began with the saleph burning down my egg factory and my chicken factory.' – I had no difficulty in accepting what he said about the factories, but I had no idea what a saleph was. Then a third party, a kind of dream commentator, explained to me that saleph was a Jewish expression for a little doctor (the underlying motifs here were Aleph, Keleph = dog; von Saalbeck, the non-Jewish vet in Amorbach). Herr Wald used the expression with the sort of ferocious familiarity universally assumed by anti-Semites when they adopt the foreign expressions still used by unassimilated Jews in the provinces. There could be no room for doubt about his attitude: he went on to say, 'Well then, and at the time the SA hadn't yet been armed.' At that point the story was interrupted and Agathe came down the stairs as if we were in Oberrad[7] and greeted Herr Wald with the cordiality she was wont to show to ordinary people she knew. However, he reacted unexpectedly by stroking her face, pinching her cheeks and speaking coarsely to her, using the familiar 'du'. I fell into a rage and Agathe tried to distract him by saying that 'The doctor is very sensitive about such things.' By now it was quite

---

[7] Oberrad is a suburb of Frankfurt south of the River Main. The Wiesengrund-Adorno family moved there in 1914, just after the outbreak of war.

clear that Herr Wald was completely drunk. I now realized that Miss Althea, our young neighbour from the other half of the house, had entered the room. (Agathe and Herr Wald were standing on the stairs.) Miss Althea wore a Slav peasant dress. I felt reassured: now that there are three of us, nothing much bad can happen. As I was on the point of deciding to throw him out, I awoke.

Los Angeles, 21 October 1942

My friend told me that he had but one musical passion: playing the double-bass. But he added that this was not a hobby he could pursue. For one thing the existing solo repertoire for the instrument was far too small. For another, his wife would not stand for his having such a large instrument in the house; it would spoil the appearance of the home.

Los Angeles, November 1942

I was with my father in London when the air raid sirens went. We went by Tube from W2 to the centre of town, and the whole story began with the fact that the train rushed at great speed all the way from Lancaster Gate to Tottenham Court Road without a single stop. At Tottenham Court Road we all got out. Everywhere there were large notices, banners actually, with the inscription: PANIC. It was as if people were being instructed to panic rather than being warned not to do so. We reached the open air right away through a side exit, but were the only ones to do so. However, I was unable to rejoice in our lucky escape. For I had the feeling that we had done something forbidden by escaping through the wrong exit, one doubt-less reserved for Tube personnel, and so for the rest of the dream I was waiting for the punishment that would inevitably overtake us. We turned southwards, in the direction of Soho, and came to a broad, friendly, but completely lifeless street. We went past a little restaurant that I instantly realized served Yugoslav food. Tables with dazzling white cloths, without a single customer, beckoned to us. A comfortable-looking manageress came to the door and urged us to enter. I felt an overwhelming desire to eat in this restaurant. My father spitefully refused to do so. It would be ridiculous, he said, to spend our precious money on such fancy food in a place like this, all because of an air raid alarm. He made me go on until we came to a manhole in the pavement. The cover was off. My father insisted that we should climb down it into the drainage system. It would be much safer there than in the restaurant.

Another night

I was talking with my girl-friend X about the erotic arts with which I thought her conversant. I asked her whether she had ever done it *par le cul*. She responded very frankly, saying that she could do it on some days, but not on others. Today was a day when it was quite impossible. This seemed quite plausible to me, but I wondered whether she was speaking the truth or whether this wasn't just a prostitute's pretext for refusing me. Then she said that she could do quite different things, more beautiful, Hungarian ones, of which I had never heard. In reply to my eager questioning, she said, 'Well, there was Babamüll, for example.' She started to explain it to me. It soon turned out that this supposed perversion was in reality a highly complicated, to me entirely opaque, but evidently illegal finance operation, something like a safe way of passing worthless cheques. I pointed out to her that this had nothing to do with the erotic techniques she had promised me. However, she stuck to her view and replied in a supercilious tone that I should pay close attention and be patient – the rest would come of its own accord. But since I had completely lost track of the connection, I despaired of ever finding out what Babamüll was.

Los Angeles, 25 November 1942

After the fall of Hitler, I had returned to Frankfurt with Gretel and Max.[8] We travelled together out to Oberrad; I can only remember the journey from when we came to the Untermain Bridge; but presumably we arrived there from the Central Station. We were driving in two cars, though sometimes it seemed to be only one and reminded me of the tram. Max drove ahead at great speed along the quay so as to get past the section from the Untermain Bridge to the Eiserne Steg [the Iron Footbridge]; it stretched out endlessly, as if the time during which I had been away had been transformed into distance, and not even the speed at which we were moving could change this. In our car I held onto a leather strap, as if it were a tram, but was shaken violently from one side to the other. The strap may even have torn loose. Gretel cried out in alarm, shouting to Max not to

---

[8] Max Horkheimer, Adorno's friend and collaborator.

drive so fast, and he slowed down right away. Then we came to the Eiserne Steg and Max turned into the crooked side street leading from Schulstrasse down to Wallstrasse. I was very puzzled: why was he making this detour and following all the turns taken by the tram? It would have been much quicker to go through Schweizerstrasse and the Mörfelder(?) Landstrasse. But it is absolutely clear, Gretel said, he was simply following the tramlines so as to have something to hold on to. – From the Lokalbahnhof on, the journey simply followed the tramlines. An inspector came on board. He was dressed in civilian clothes and looked extremely distinguished. With his small but bushy moustache and his unusually clear blue eyes, he resembled an older, aristocratic, higher Prussian official. I at once entered into conversation with him and felt the need to make all sorts of confessions to him. These were connected with the next stop, the Wendelsplatz. In my childhood, I said, I used to try and annoy the tram conductors by intentionally mispronouncing the name of the stop in an affected way. Instead of Wendelsplatz, I would say Wendélls Platz, with the stress on the last syllable. It made it sound like an irritating, incomprehensible foreign word. I only did this to make the hostile conductor lose his temper with my arrogance, since no one would venture to correct me, the educated youth. Needless to say, I knew perfectly well that Wendelsplatz was the proper pronunciation. However, the inspector pointed out amiably that I was mistaken; in reality it was called Wendellsweg, according to the writer Hardy or Haldane or Harder or Hardart, who had written Tristan. 'In that case, it must be Hardart',

I said, 'since he owns the liveliest cafeterias in New York.'
'Quite right', the inspector said. 'But he also owns the
Natural History Museum and the Art History Museum.'

Los Angeles, beginning of December 1942

I was present at a large, unusually lavish banquet. It was
being held in an impressive building, probably the
Palmengarten in Frankfurt. The rooms and the tables were
lit only by candles, and this made it difficult to find one's
way to the main table or to the smaller tables that had been
laid for several people. I struck out in search of my place
on my own, walking through endless corridors. I passed
one table where there was a very loud, emotional discussion between two men from a famous banking family. It
concerned a particular sort of very young little lobsters
that are cooked in such a way that – as with American soft
crabs – you can eat the shells. Someone explained that they
were cooked in this way so as to preserve the taste of the
shells, the best bit. One banker eloquently defended this
point of view; the other was thinking about his health and
hurled abuse at his relative for being so unreasonable. In
my dream I did not really know what to make of this. On
the one hand, I felt it was undignified to quarrel about food;
on the other hand, I could not help admiring the sight of
two such powerful men so openly and unashamedly dis-
playing their own vulgar materialism. Apart from that, the
banquet never progressed beyond the hors d'oeuvres. I
finally discovered my place without any trouble. Beside the
place setting there was a card with my name on it, and I was
surprised that it seemed to be expecting me. I was even

more surprised that my table companion was to be a swanky woman I already knew very well and who was approaching from a different direction. The various hors d'oeuvres were now served. There were different ones for women and men. The latter were served very strong, spicy, tasty dishes. I remember that they included some tiny cold cutlets with a red sauce. The ladies' hors d'oeuvres were vegetarian, but of the most exquisite sort: heart of palm, leek, roast chicory – all this seemed the very essence of refinement. To my utter horror, however, my neighbour attracted everyone's attention by loudly summoning the waiter as if she were in a restaurant, whereas it was accepted here that, in view of the lavish entertainment, it was not possible to ask for anything. She said that she wanted not just the hors d'oeuvres meant for the women, but also those intended for the men. She would not put up with being discriminated against. Without waiting for the response to her complaint, I woke up.

Los Angeles, 10 January 1943

I was visiting an American brothel. It was a large, distinguished-looking establishment. Even so, anyone who entered had to undergo endless formalities. He had to register, fill in a questionnaire, and speak to the madam who ran the place, her assistant and finally the woman in charge of sales. By the time it came to making a choice, it turned out that the administration occupied almost the entire brothel, so that the girls were left with nothing more than a small, untidy communal room. It reminded me of the hotel room of some travelling virtuoso where the unmade bed has to serve as a seat for the all too numerous visitors. The girls felt very cramped. There were no more than five or six of them, all either unprepossessing or downright ugly. Only one of them seemed pretty to me; she was cowering on the bed, naked but otherwise quite harmless. She was called Eads. (Motif: Wildgans's Sonnets to Ead. The previous evening I had written a sonnet for R.) She had only one flaw: she was made entirely of glass, or perhaps from the same elastic, transparent synthetic material that my new braces are made from. One could even see through her head. She was not actually dead, but had a sort of life, though not a real one: it seemed to be connected with the suppleness of the material. I couldn't make up my mind whether to have her. Of course, I did not fail to notice that the woman in charge of the girls was herself very attractive, although somewhat plump. I explained to her politely that I trusted she would not feel insulted, but her position in the brothel made me feel that she would be free from prejudices, and that since she was so much more attractive than her protégées I would like to ask her if she wouldn't like to do it with me (motifs: the madam in the Sphinx in Paris). She seemed flattered, but during the elaborate negotiations that followed, the dream went dark.

Los Angeles, 16 January 1943, early morning

I was lying in bed with two delightful women. One of them was small, delicate, with round, very firm breasts, and she was distinguished by great devotion and tenderness, which I at once noted with gratitude. The other was tall, slender, 'good looking' – except that from behind she had strangely protruding bones. She reminded me of Frau von R. Both of them had wonderful perfumed skin and I remember that I paid them a quite fatuous compliment, saying that 'at long last I had found some genuine high-class tarts.' However, we never progressed as far as intercourse – something I never dream of explicitly, any more than I dream of death – but only to kissing and indecent fondling. I was more interested in the smaller woman; the tall one developed a certain resistance. The smaller one, who was on my side – and how happy this made me feel! – declared that she would take me with her to the Beverly Hills Hotel; she had an entire apartment to herself there and could receive men there at any time without any difficulty. After that, and as I turned my attentions more towards her, the tall girl became more accommodating. The room, incidentally, was the kind of spacious room typical of an elegant summer resort like Bar Harbor. Suddenly, there was a frightful din. People rushed in, X and F. W. in the lead. X wore a cap as a kind of proletarian uniform. Both of them confronted me like judges from the Party. This took the form of shouting the same word at me in turn in a tone of furious indignation: 'Barbarians – barbarians – barbarians'. By this they meant the women and myself. It now became clear that the two women were both former wives of L.'s, and that L. still had some sort of claims on them. At the same time, however, the smaller woman seemed also to be identical with Frau X, though without resembling her in the least. It also emerged that a man, my best friend, had taken part in the preceding events, and the smaller woman now sought protection from him. I was gripped by straightforward fear of the consequences of the scene. L., his eyes wild with uncontrollable fury, kept on repeating: 'I demand an explanation.' Feeling desperate, I became entangled in a legalistic discussion with him in which I tried to prove to him that the scene meant nothing since intercourse had not taken place. Without any great sense of hope, I awoke.

Los Angeles, 15 February 1943

Agathe appeared to me in a dream, saying something to the effect that 'Karl Kraus was the wittiest and most brilliant of all writers. You can only really see that from the notebooks that were found in his posthumous writings. They contain the most indescribable bons mots. I'll give you an example. One day, an anonymous admirer sent him a giant rice pudding [*Reisauflauf* = soufflé]. The pudding itself was not a success; it boiled over and the grains of rice formed a lumpy mess. Kraus became cross and referred to "This riot [*Volksauflauf*] of a rice pudding".' Awoke (in the morning), laughing out loud at this supposedly brilliant witticism.

Los Angeles, 28 February 1943

Alexander Granach[9] arranged for a reading from his novel consisting of a number of stories. The reading took place

---

[9] Born in Poland, Alexander Granach (1893–1945) was a leading German stage and film actor in the 1920s and 1930s, and later made a name for himself on Broadway and in Hollywood as a character actor (e.g. in films such as *Ninotchka* with Greta Garbo and *Hangmen Also Die*).

in a large hall – that of the Saalbau in Frankfurt? – I was present with my mother. She seemed to be extremely old, tiny, but also unusually quick in her movements ('Les petites vieilles').[10] Saying that she wanted to avoid making a fuss, she persuaded me to stay in a function room which was joined to the hall through connecting doors and which extended it at the end away from the platform; so it was a sort of foyer. I told my mother that we couldn't possibly hear anything there and that we had to go into the main hall. She reluctantly agreed. We then did so, but instead of entering down the middle aisle dividing the rows of seats, we went along the side. My mother thought that even this drew too much attention to us and she insisted on a peculiar zigzag route: every time we came to a side door, we had to exit through it and walk along the outside until the next door, when we went back in, and so on, until we had walked the entire length of the hall. We finally found seats quite close to the platform. They were marked 'reserved' and hardly anyone was sitting there, so we ended up attracting attention after all. The only member of the audience I knew was Jemnitz, who nodded to me vigorously, giving every sign that he was delighted to see me again. I said he must be here because he too is called Alexander. (NB Alexander is also my father's second name.) In the meanwhile, Granach appeared on the platform. However, he scarcely resembled Granach and in fact looked much more like Toni Maaskoff. Only then did I become aware of the peculiar nature of the platform. It looked a little like the

[10] The title of a poem by Baudelaire.

battlemented lookout platform of a tower above which the spire rises up still higher. Granach, who had evidently arrived late, began to speak in the half-empty hall. He said he found it quite impossible to decide in what order to read the texts he had chosen. He would therefore have to ask his friends who had organized the reading to come up on the platform to discuss the matter and come to a decision. Muttering in the audience. This was followed by a kind of silent pantomime between Max and myself – we were sitting quite far apart from each other. Each of us made pleading gestures to the other to be the one to go up on the platform, or at least to be the first to go. Finally, we both went, together with a number of others whom we did not know. On the platform we were told that the consultation could not take place there in full sight of the audience; we would have to go to the top of the spire, which rose up far above the open part of the stage (the platform had now turned into a stage). So we climbed up. It was very steep, difficult and dangerous, something halfway between a spiral staircase and an Alpine chimney. Having reached the top, we found that there was scarcely any room for us inside the spire. We had to come down again. I was now gripped by panic, I had the feeling it was one of those situations where you can climb up, but not climb down again. The dream then skipped the downward climb. I did not realize where I was until I found myself back on the platform. In the meantime, the audience was becoming very restive and the sequence of readings had still not been settled. I felt I was in a desperate situation in which something just had to be done right away, no matter what. So I told Granach that the only thing that would work would be something forceful, something that would utterly overwhelm the audience. He should at once read out the pogrom story of Rachmonesl and Gott-zum-Dank (a story that really exists). He seemed to take my advice and, somewhat reassured by this, I went on sleeping.

16 April 1943

Next Tuesday old Hahn has his eighty-fifth birthday. I dreamt: what can one give to old Hahn on his eighty-fifth birthday, something he might find useful? – Answer: a guide to the kingdom of the dead.

Los Angeles, 12 May 1943

After Luli's first visit to us I had a dream. I was at a party that was spread out over a number of rooms and at which a lot of alcohol was being consumed. I encountered an elderly, elegantly dressed gentleman – either I bumped into him or else I trod on his toe. His twirled moustache seemed familiar to me. I apologized politely, perhaps too eagerly. The gentleman angrily turned his back on me. Then someone else came up to me, a negro with a reddish-brown face, somewhat slit, almond-shaped eyes and a rather shaggy beard with side whiskers. He was officiously eager and revealed to me that he was the gentleman's adjutant (both were in plain clothes). He told me that the gentleman was Kaiser Wilhelm and that I had committed a terrible faux pas. Not the fact that I had trodden on his toe – he would not take such a thing amiss. But the strictest rules of etiquette laid down that no one in any circumstances should ever speak first to the Kaiser. The Kaiser adhered passionately to this rule. By apologizing I had offended against it. In the final analysis, however, it was not unforgivable and he, the adjutant, would do everything in his power to smooth things out.

Summer 1943

A few weeks ago I dreamt that someone had asked me: 'How could someone like you possibly enjoy going to boring parties!' Without hesitation I replied: 'Because I so like the smell of powder.'

Los Angeles, 22 November 1943

I dreamt that I was reading an essay by Herwarth Walden in the arts section of the *Frankfurter Zeitung*. It was on Shakespeare. He maintained that some of the least esteemed comedies, and especially *The Comedy of Errors*, were actually his most important works, and that that play in particular was the key to Shakespeare as a whole. Its theme was resemblance. In that play Shakespeare had treated the problem of mimesis. The essay went on to explain how he had done so. Excited by this, I telephoned Gubler to congratulate him on publishing the article.[11]

---

[11] Herwarth Walden (1878–1941) was a writer associated with expressionism, but achieved much greater prominence as the publisher of the expressionist magazine *Der Sturm*. He later became a communist and emigrated to Russia, where he disappeared. Friedrich Traugott Gubler, a Swiss, became editor of the arts section of the *Frankfurter Zeitung* in 1931.

The previous night

At a reception given by a society lady in L. A. with Gretel
and Norah. A long line of ragged children and hoodlums[12]
filed past the hostess. I whispered something to Norah about
these strange figures. She immediately said out loud: 'My
friend Teddie doesn't like it here. There are too many Reds.'
I made desperate efforts to correct the misunderstanding
both in her eyes and in those of the assembled company.

Los Angeles, beginning of January 1944

Dieterle has written a play entitled 'Bake Little Hegel
Lambs'![13]

Los Angeles, end of March 1944

In an arena, under my command, a large number of Nazis
were to be executed. They were to be beheaded. There was
a hitch for some reason or other. To simplify matters it was
decided to smash the skulls of each of the delinquents indi-
vidually with a pickaxe. I was then informed that the
victims had been overwhelmed by an indescribable terror
at the prospect of this uncertain and excruciating form of
execution. I was myself so disgusted by this atrocity that
I awoke feeling physically sick.

[12] Adorno used the English word.

[13] Wilhelm Dieterle (1893–1972) was a well-known film actor in
Germany during the age of silent movies (Murnau's *Faust*) who
then became famous in exile in Hollywood, where he co-
directed *A Midsummer Night's Dream* with Max Reinhardt and,
later, *The Hunchback of Notre Dame*. He was friendly with
Adorno in California.

Los Angeles, 2 April 1944

Gretel said to me: 'I now know who Y's latest lover is. It is Mannesmann, the inventor of the Mannesmann pipes.'

Los Angeles, 8 June 1944

I dreamt that, in great excitement, Agathe and Maria[14] together told me the latest Louische story. It consisted of two sentences which also occurred in the dream: 'Louische, would you like to drink a glass of water?' – 'No, thank you, I shall be drowned this evening anyway.' Woke up laughing.[15]

Los Angeles, 1 August 1944

I was due once again to be executed – like Pierrot lunaire. This time, like a pig. I was to be thrown into boiling water. I was assured that it would be completely painless, since I would be dead before I realized what was happening. I was in fact quite free of fear, merely somewhat surprised by a technical detail: immediately after the scalding, cold water would be let in, as with a hot bath. So I was thrown into the cauldron. To my ineffable astonishment, however, I did not die right away, but nor was I in any pain. However, probably because of the additional water that had been let in, I did feel a pressure that seemed to increase inexorably. I realized that if I did not succeed in waking up right away, I really would die. Managed to wake up after huge efforts

---

[14] Adorno's mother.

[15] Louische or Lujche is a fictional character who is the protagonist in some sketches Adorno wrote over a number of years.

(physically in a poor state, bad neuralgia, in a condition between life and death, after dreaming of a visit from Luise Rainer that lasted until deep into the night).[16]

Los Angeles, 10 August 1944

Together with Luise Rainer I went to a kind of press ball in Europe. It was held in an opera house, in Frankfurt or Vienna. But the building was badly damaged, probably as the consequence of an air raid, and in fact had no roof so that it looked more like a decorative façade. The celebrities present also seemed to look rather the worse for wear. One of them, whom I knew, seemed to have turned into an old man. L. slipped into the party, mingling unobtrusively in her street clothes with people who were all dressed up or wearing masks. No one recognized her. We too took no notice of the party but were totally immersed in each other. I remember the utterly unembarrassed, open way in which she looked straight into my eyes. Suddenly, we found ourselves in a room where music was being played, but, as soon as it started, L. stood up gently but firmly and I left the room with her. The whole event turned into a love scene that was completely shameless, without being exhibitionistic. It was like a victory over those present, a frank act of disappearance, an unconscious challenge to the

---

[16] Luise Rainer (1910–), a German-Jewish film actress, became well known in Germany before the war and made a successful career in the USA after Hitler came to power. She won two Oscars (*The Great Ziegfeld*, *The Good Earth*) and was briefly married to the American writer Clifford Odets.

world. Woke up with a feeling of happiness that was still there when I phoned her up.

Los Angeles, 26 August 1944

I dreamt that I was shaving with a contraption that was as simple as it was remarkable. It consisted merely of a U-shaped thin glass tube, less than one centimetre in diameter. I stuck one end of it in my mouth and passed the other end over my cheeks, while it removed all the hair without any sort of knife and without my feeling anything. Then I noticed that at the shaving end of the tube a yellowish liquid had formed with hairs floating in it. I did not know whether this liquid was an acid that removed the hairs or just my own saliva. But I felt a sudden anxiety that the liquid might flow into my mouth and that I might swallow the little hairs, which seemed highly dangerous to me. I woke up choked with disgust.

Los Angeles, 3 September 1944

I lay awake a long time because feelings of sadness and disappointment were going through my mind. A car raced past the house; I could still hear the screeching of the brakes as it reached San Vincente Boulevard. Immediately after this, I dreamt that one of the little metal airships, of the kind that flew around New York before the war carrying advertisements, had gone up just by our house, but it had a roaring engine just like a plane, and it flew at tremendous speed so close to the roof that I was afraid it would take the house with it. This cannot end well, I thought, and just then the airship which had already reached a considerable height began to wobble and went into a spin. It turned over and crashed into a field. I went towards it, supposedly to help, or to fetch help, but in reality out of curiosity and especially to stare at the victims. But before I could manage to tell anyone about it – I myself remained at a respectful distance – a number of people dressed like technicians were already standing round the wreckage, clearing away the remains. They even pulled out a man who was mortally injured, but still alive. While the men seemed to be engaged in rescuing him, they tugged at him furiously – their act of rescue was indistinguishable from the Maquisards' acts of revenge against people who had fraternized with the Germans, a subject of which the newspapers are full. The dying man came to and cried out 'Water, water', and then 'I'm dying of thirst', repeated several times. Utterly unmoved, I thought that in this situation no one would say, 'I'm dying of thirst.' He had just seen that this was common among people dying of burns and that was why he kept on repeating it. Then I felt sure that he had died and so kept on sleeping peacefully.

Berkeley, 17 October 1944

Subsequently transcribed from a postcard to Gretel. I was at a party with several members of the Guermantes family:[17] Oriane, Charlus and the Princess. Oriane looked sensational, but was wearing spectacles. She greeted me with the words 'My cousin Marie' – i.e. the Princess – 'wanted to invite you to try out her new vodka. However,

[17] From Proust's series of novels *À la recherche du temps perdu*.

I told her that you were a wine connoisseur, but not an expert on spirits. That is why she cancelled the invitation. But she is so stupid that that you didn't miss anything.' Palamède, a handsome, elderly man, kept on smiling insolently and then the Princess began a conversation which I have forgotten.

Fragments, Los Angeles, October 1944

There was a large party at which Trotsky was present. He was the centre of a group of disciples to whom he was lecturing in an animated and somewhat authoritarian fashion. The question arose of whether one should speak to him. I voted in favour, adding that one should not talk politics, but simply that it would be inelegant to cut such a renowned guest. – In an otherwise completely destroyed German city, I saw a giant, blackened church spire. Overjoyed, I exclaimed, 'So the cathedral is still standing', only to be told that this was not Frankfurt, this was Magdeburg. – A very pretty brunette kissed me with great skill. But she insisted on keeping her cigarette in her mouth during the kiss.

Los Angeles, 23 November 1944

A sentence: 'The Myth of the Twentieth Century is Lujche.'

Los Angeles, 20 January 1945

Another brothel dream. It took place in Paris. But the house had the size and height of a New York skyscraper, such as the RCA Building. I found myself in a crowd of men and women. Apart from Gretel – of whose presence I was aware without actually seeing her – my mother and Maidon were also there.[18] We went to the upper storeys in a giant express lift. It rushed upwards for a long time without stopping. It must have been the sixtieth floor at least before we stopped, but care had been taken to prevent anyone from identifying the number of the floor. During the journey I was struck by the very pretty, dark-haired Jewish girl who was operating the lift. I asked her if she knew her way around the brothel. She answered politely but firmly that she had never been up there, kept herself to herself and in general led a very strict life. 'That's the only way to cope with things like that.' – The floor where we stopped seemed to be vast, even though it also reminded me of a Berlin boarding house. We passed through a number of rooms before reaching a large reception room. It was all decorated in yellow, but very elegantly and decently. When I pointed this out to my mother she made a very blasé comment after the fashion of a woman of the world – it was nothing special, in her youth she had seen lots of places like that. The rather sparse collection of people in the room seemed to be waiting for more people to come, rather like in a guided tour. Next to my mother there sat a puritanically dressed woman staring doggedly; she reminded me of Frau K. M. It was the brothel keeper. My mother said in a low voice that she knew her well, although the woman gave no sign of recognizing her. My mother added that already in her youth the wicked

---

[18] Maidon is Maidon Horkheimer, Max Horkheimer's wife.

woman's family had a bad reputation. After a while, another woman belonging to the house spoke up and welcomed us. She was tall, dressed in black (with a white collar and cuffs), and looked somewhat blurred. She reminded me of Frau Fischer, my parents' landlady. She explained that the guiding principle of her establishment was that the guests should entertain themselves. Everyone could contribute something; a first-rate piano was at our disposal. Each guest had been given a bell. Anyone who wanted someone else to perform had only to ring his or her bell. She just wanted to warn us against any disorder; the general lectures often gave rise to an unbearable noise and everyone had to suffer. She went on to speak about Heidegger – she may have recommended his writings for reading aloud. This provoked a storm of indignation among a group of Jewish clothing manufacturers or *Aufbau* readers.[19] It was an impertinence, they said, to expect them to put up with such difficult and demanding reading-matter in a place like this. Self-righteously protesting in the style of the boiling soul of the people, the group left the brothel. The whole party now set out on a sort of tour of the premises. They arrived first at a spacious forecourt laid out as a cafeteria; tables and chairs gleamed metallically. After this, there was only artificial light. Maidon announced that she would not go any further, she would stay where she was, and she sat down at a little table together with my mother and some others. They were

[19] The *Aufbau* was a German-language émigré newspaper published in New York from 1934 on. It survives to this day.

joined by a few ladies belonging to the establishment, attractive but dressed in deep mourning. I was pursued by an importunate waiter who kept repeating, 'Vous prenez un seltzer, Monsieur, vous prenez un seltzer.'[20] (The woman who spoke earlier had also spoken in French, but had lapsed into German, perhaps when she realized that the party consisted mainly of émigrés.) I turned to a pimp who was employed there and who looked like Adolphe Menjou, and asked whether they were not going to parade the girls so that we could choose. He replied that this had often been suggested – most recently by Dr M. In this establishment, however, everyone had to fend for himself. We then arrived at the inner sanctum. It most resembled the sleeping cars on American trains. A narrow corridor passed between the berths which, however, instead of solid walls had red curtains, as if they had only recently been put up. All the berths were occupied; conversations could be heard coming from some of them. I was irritated at the thought that here one was forced to take the first girl available, however repulsive, and that there was no freedom of choice. However, it then struck me that the berths were more like improvised theatre dressing-rooms than sleeping compartments. The curtains were only loosely drawn, not firmly closed. I cautiously looked through a gap. I could not see whether a man was inside or not, but I glimpsed a tall woman, fully clothed in a dark-brown fur coat, standing in front of the dressing-room mirror and putting on her make-up. It was the same scene in the next berth and in all

---

[20] 'Would you like some soda water, Monsieur?'

the berths that I glanced into. At last, an old French gentleman with a pointed white beard like that of Anatole France
burst out of one of the berths in a rage, but said nothing.
At that moment I realized that I was still clinging to my old,
shabby, unmodern velvet or plush hat – at any rate, it was
a sort of artist's hat. I blamed my hat for the frustrating
outcome of my adventure, and awoke.

Los Angeles, 31 March 1945

After I heard the radio announcement of Eisenhower's call
for the Germans to lay down their arms, I fell asleep in the
afternoon and dreamt I was in South Germany, in a large
room with a bay window looking out onto a market place,
in Würzburg or Amorbach. It was a warm night – much
warmer than it ever is in the German summer. The sky was
a deep greeny blue, of a shade only seen in theatre decora-
tions. It contained a myriad little shining stars which,
however, were all identical with each other and arranged in
a symmetrical order. I turned my head to get a better view
of the show, but when I did so, the wallpaper-like star
pattern moved before my eyes, like in a film. In my dream
I thought: this is impossible, the stars are not all the same
size, nor are they arranged symmetrically. So I concentrated on looking at them more closely. To my delight I discovered a group of stars, a constellation, which stood out
from the general pattern. It consisted of larger and brighter
stars. Admittedly, each of them seemed more like an electric light. At the same time, the efforts I was making to look
at them and my scepticism in the midst of my dream made
me wake up. The entire thing can have lasted no more than

a second. The dream made me feel *exceedingly* happy; highly colourful.

Los Angeles, 14 July 1945

Execution scene. Whether the victims were fascists or antifascists remained unclear. At all events, it was a crowd of naked, athletic young men. But they looked just like their own busts: metallic green. The execution proceeded like a self-service operation. Everyone went up into the automated guillotine in no discernible order, and came out again without a head, staggered on for a few steps and then fell down dead. I remember a younger person, a boy, who as if in fun pushed his way forward to the entrance of the guillotine in front of a larger man entering from the side, as if eager to be executed first. I observed the movements of the headless men and thought that I should try to find out whether they were still conscious and whether, as seemed to me to be the case, they took care to avoid falling down on top of one another. I watched one youth closely. After a few steps he went head over heels several times as if he were performing somersaults, and then fell down on top of another corpse. All without a word or any other sound. I watched without any emotion, but woke up with an erection. (They went to the guillotine one after the other, as if they were practising. In fact, my main impression was of a gymnastic exercise.)

Los Angeles, 17 August 1945

A very black Friday. I had a dream weeks ago, and what I dreamt seemed so crucial that it was as if everything depended upon it and as if I had penetrated to the inner-most secret of the futility of existence. Then I forgot the dream. A few days ago, in the depths of my worst depression since the winter months of 1942–3, I had the same dream again, or, rather, I had a dream in which I remembered fragments of the first dream. I have forgotten most of it, but I want to retain the pitiful vestiges I can remember in the hope that one day I shall perhaps remember more. I was travelling to Vienna to visit Alban Berg, whom I had arranged to see for a day or two. On my arrival I learned of his death. Either I received a telegram or I rang up and was given the news over the telephone. Without thinking about where I was going to sleep, I started walking quickly – just as one does on hearing the worst possible news; one doesn't think about means of transport, of taking a taxi, but just sets out on foot, as if in extreme circumstances one's own body were the only certainty. I walked aimlessly in a giant arc around the city, roughly along the Gürtel (even though I did not start out from the Westbahnhof where I normally arrived). Nothing of what I saw reminded me of Vienna: brown houses and sheds, perhaps made of wood, predominated. It was like walking up to a wall of rain, but the sun lay on top of it and lit up the haze as if to show me the way. (I felt as if I had to fight my way against a powerful pressure, which, however, I managed to overcome.) Splashes of damp greenery gleamed and I had the feeling that what I saw was extremely beautiful. But, at the same time, I knew that it was all illusion, everything was lost now that he was dead, and nothing could make it good. I awoke thinking that

I had never succeeded in getting over Alban's death and that his death had never become quite real to me until I had this dream.

Postscript to this dream

I often have a similar dream about *Paris*. I take a long walk far out along the left bank of the Seine. Unlike the real river, the river in my dream has countless bends. At one bend, suddenly, unexpectedly, I glimpse the entire panorama of the city stretched out before me, but compressed into a miniature space. It looks like a giant, old-fashioned set of fortifications, with a few large industrial complexes (including two matching ones) in the middle. I know the names of every building, every street and every park. They are the familiar ones: the Madeleine, the Grands Boulevards, the Luxemburg and, especially, Notre Dame and the Île Saint Louis. But all the buildings that bear these names are quite unlike those I know and for the most part they seem to have been replaced by much older ones. I am aware of the difference even while I am dreaming, perhaps with the undercurrent that this was not the real Paris after all. The whole scene is lit up by an eclipse like the image of Toledo in El Greco. The whole scene is shot through with the same hopeless feeling of sorrow as my visit to Vienna.

Los Angeles, 19 September 1945

My father asked me, 'Do you know the origin of the name Dreyfus?' I replied, 'Presumably, it comes from some utensil in the Jewish Temple, a "tripod" [*Dreifuß*].' 'You are mistaken', my father declared. He went on to explain that, in Frankfurt during the Middle Ages, there was a regulation according to which a limit was placed on the height of houses. Now there were individual houses that had been built three feet [*drei Fuß*] higher, thanks to the existence of certain privileges. A number of Frankfurt Jews took the name Dreyfuß after these houses. Only a few months before, he himself, my father, that is, had had the opportunity to acquire one of these houses or else to raise the house in Schöne Aussicht by three feet. It would only have cost 60,000 Marks. However, he had missed the opportunity and now it was gone for ever.[21]

Los Angeles, 6 October 1945

Two dreams, one after the other. L. L. had a second child, a little daughter. It was a tiny, ugly baby with a crumpled face and was lying in bed with G., its mother. Next to the bed stood D., who had been changed back into a child and who was abusing me with such epithets as 'You idiot!', half in jest. I took very little notice. On the other hand, I heard that in New York a major criminal, who was in fact a very evil character, had been sentenced to death and was to be executed. However, L. felt indignant about it and wished to prevent the execution at any cost. For this reason, he had forced G. to give the state governor her diamond ring as

[21] This is of course a 'dream' etymology. It is now believed that the name Dreyfus is a toponym whose origins can be traced back to the Rhineland town of Trier, presumably through its French name of Trèves.

a bribe to call off the execution. Still in the dream, I discussed the matter with G. I began by praising L.'s noble desire to wish to make such a sacrifice, however misplaced. But then I also had some doubts, and said that he was only doing this because he wanted to imitate M., whom he knew to be a passionate opponent of the death penalty. Moreover, the sacrifice would be made by his wife.

The second, much more chaotic dream: there was to be a kind of academic celebration for a historian or politician. The company present at the event included Max and women such as B. and J., the latter having shrunk to the size of a dwarf. She looked up at me, flirting provocatively; while I, very put off, beat a retreat on the pretext that I had an infectious form of neuralgia. The entire company was brought down to the ground in a goods lift. There was no room in it for me so I remained on the upper floor. Then the scene changed. There was a classroom full of children, with a high-school teacher (who in reality was not a high-school teacher at all, but only a primary-school teacher), and an adjoining room. Max, dressed in a morning coat, was striding up and down expectantly on the forecourt. Hanns Eisler sat in the room entirely on his own and in a pitiful state. The high-school teacher went up to him and asked about a man who had played a crucial role as an ordinary soldier in an episode in the Thirty Years' War. I knew that the man was called Natier or Napier. Hanns, however, was unable to utter a single word. It was obvious that all the answers that the high-school teacher was drilling into him were connected with the specialized field of the man who was due to be honoured. After Hanns's failure to respond, the high-school teacher fell to cursing, saying that such ignorance would inevitably turn the entire ceremony into a disaster. I attempted to enter the class-room. But my white silk jacket got caught in a door or a cupboard, and whenever I released it, it immediately got caught again the moment I freed it. Then I had an idea. I wanted to suggest to the teacher that, instead of naming historical events and then to ask for names and dates connected with it, he should start with the names and dates and then ask what events they were associated with. Then everyone would know the answers. But before I could properly present my ideas, I woke up.

Los Angeles, 14 October 1945

It was a small party at the Dieterles, with a table laid in the shape of a horse shoe so that there was a fairly large vacant space in the middle. From what I remember, those present included Gretel and Lou Eisler. Lou said that Gottfried Reinhardt was there with his young wife.[22] I did not see him, but I did notice a rather voluptuous lady with a very low neckline, wearing a dress the colour of raw silk. Someone – not I – said that must be she, she looked just like a youthful version of Salka.[23] The lady picked up this

[22] Lou Eisler was the second wife of the composer Hanns Eisler. Gottfried Reinhardt was the son of Max Reinhardt and a film director in his own right, both in Germany and later in Hollywood.

[23] Salka is Salka Viertel, the actress and screenwriter. She was the sister of Adorno's great friend the pianist Eduard Steuermann. She married Berthold Viertel, the theatre director and writer,

remark and attacked me loudly from across the table, as if I had been guilty of making an extremely tactless remark. 'You might just as well call me Luli Lehn', she said cuttingly. This was the cue for a flood of highly malicious gossip about Luli. Cabaret tart was one of the terms that was to be heard. I felt an irresistible impulse to leap to her defence, so I went into the empty space and called out: 'We are close friends of Countess G. and I will not stand for anything unkind being said about her in my presence.' I felt uncomfortable while I was speaking. I had the feeling that I was only showing off, and that in fact we weren't such close friends any more. Nevertheless, I was unable to desist from my tirade. To my amazement, my speech was well received. One lady said, 'It is really very nice to see such a semi-countess find such a knight to leap to her defence.' However, another lady said that she thought this very strange. Luli had told her she had scarcely seen us, and on one occasion she had said grumpily that today she had to visit friends in the Wolfswiesenhöhle. – Gap in the dream. A young man came up to me and as a joke tied a mask made of paper serviettes and a fool's cap on my head. I was unable to join in the joke and felt only rage and a wish to destroy something. I tore off the mask and tried to tie it on him, making very hostile comments all the while. Gretel said my behaviour was impossible. At that point, Charlotte Dieterle appeared, perhaps trying to smooth things over,

---

and moved to California with him. Her salon was a focal point for German émigrés in Hollywood. She was a close friend of Greta Garbo and wrote the screenplays for *Anna Karenina* and *Queen Christina*, among other films.

but she was very indistinct so that I didn't really see her properly. At that moment I realized that all these events were allusions to the desperate woman I loved and who did not appear in the dream at all (her name!). I suddenly recalled the verses from the *Winterreise*, 'I have committed no crime – / Why should I flee mankind?'[24] I knew that everything I did in this dream had self-destruction as its aim. But the dream itself desired to teach me about this and cure me.

Los Angeles, 29 October 1945

Visit to Anatole France. A highly elegant lift – black as ebony – brought me up to his room or office. The door was ajar; the room, a corner room all in red. I knocked and France told me to come in right away. He was a tall, slim man in his early forties, smoothly shaven, with brown hair, quite unlike any of his pictures. He wore a black, strikingly well-tailored velvet jacket. The conversation turned first to his latest novel, whose title I still knew when I woke up, but then instantly forgot. This was followed by a discussion with sharply diverging views, polite, but uncomfortable. Then my glance fell on two photographs. One represented France himself, the second showed a lady very elegantly dressed in an old-fashioned way, with a plunging neckline, whom I instantly recognized as an actress and whose outstanding beauty I greatly admired. It was the writer's mother. 'I too am a child of the theatre', I said to him: 'my mother was a celebrated singer.' At this moment the

---

[24] From 'Der Wegweiser' [The Signpost] in Schubert's *Winterreise*.

transformation took place. France, evidently delighted by my confession, changed before my eyes into a young, highly seductive woman with provocative breasts which pressed hard against the V-shaped neckline of her black lace dress, and long, black silk stockings. I kissed the top of her breasts, her mouth, played with her legs, and it was settled that from now on she would be my mistress. She asked whether she could come with me to the opera the following Tuesday – it was now Friday – to *The Marriage of Figaro*. I agreed enthusiastically. She said she wanted to go to the matinée, for children. This put me in a highly embarrassing position. I tried to explain to her that I had already invited Maurice Ravel to that very same children's performance. I gave her a highly rational account of the latter's mental illness from which I concluded that he was only capable of enjoying performances for children, and this explained why I could not cancel the arrangement. But I had the feeling that this explanation did not go down well and woke up with the fear that my new love had already passed its highpoint before it could even blossom properly.

Los Angeles, 4 February 1946

Strong feelings of oppression, evidently connected with illness. I was part of a larger group that had assembled to bid farewell to Laval, before his execution. It resembled a family scene, with kisses and tears. For my part, I spoke quietly with the delinquent; he wore black and a white tie. I felt it was my duty. Just before the procession was about to move off to the execution, however, I was overwhelmed by the sense of his utter forsakenness. I went up to him;

however, he only noticed me after he had been given a nudge by people standing around him. I grasped his hand and said, 'Au revoir, Pierre', and he thanked me. The procession then marched on through a kind of mountain and valley railway – artificially laid out – and on into the depths. It was supposed to be possible to gain a clear sight of him from particular vantage points. But almost from the very beginning I could no longer see him at all – it was almost as if the procession had gone completely astray. In contrast, my mother, who had also been present among those taking their leave, started to sing Mahler's *Kindertotenlieder* in a clear, youthful voice. And what she sang was 'Wenn dein Mütterlein' [When your mother comes in at the door]. I followed the entire melody. Suddenly, while still dreaming, I understood the meaning of her lament for the dead: I was Laval, one of the people who betrayed the French to the Germans. I awoke with indescribable feelings of terror and a wildly racing pulse.

Berkeley, 24 March 1946

During the night before the decisive quarrel with Charlotte, I had a dream. As I awoke, I remembered her final words: 'I am the martyr of happiness.'

Los Angeles, 18 February 1948

I dreamt I owned a voluminous, illustrated, luxury edition of a book on surrealism, and the dream really consisted in the exact description of one of the illustrations. It depicted a large hall. The rear of its side wall on the left – far from the observer – was occupied by a clumsy fresco that I instantly recognized as a 'German Hunting Scene'. Green as in Trübner predominated.[25] Its subject was a giant aurochs which had reared up on his hind legs and seemed to be dancing. But the entire length of the hall was filled with a series of objects that were precisely aligned. Next to the picture was a stuffed aurochs, roughly the size of the one in the picture, and likewise standing on its hind legs. Then, a living aurochs in the same pose, still very large, but somewhat smaller. The same pose was adopted also by a succession of animals, first, two not entirely distinct brown animals, presumably bears, then another two smaller, live aurochs, and lastly, two ordinary cattle. The entire ensemble seemed to be under the command of a child, a very graceful girl dressed in a very short grey silk dress and long grey silk stockings. This child led the parade much like a conductor. There was a signature at the bottom of the painting: Claude Debussy. (I had this dream while I was writing the long essay on Stravinsky for the *Philosophy of Modern Music*.)

Los Angeles, 14 March 1948

I had had a lot to drink in the evening and knew that I would be able to sleep it off on Sunday. So it was a night full of dreams. I can remember two dreams. First, I recollected a film script that I wanted to give to Fritz Lang (with whom we lunched today). It was to be called 'The Forgotten

---

[25] Presumably the painter Wilhelm Trübner (1851–1917), known for his somewhat grandiose scenes of landscapes and buildings in a realist or impressionist style.

Princess'. It concerned a princess who had no function in the modern world and is therefore forgotten. She turns to the hotel industry, experiences all sorts of conflicts and ends up marrying a head waiter.

The second dream is much more disturbing. I had been given a child to torture, a delightful, twelve-year old boy. He had been spread out on a little apparatus that was positioned at an angle so that his delicate body was everywhere exposed. I began by boxing his ears and kissing him on the mouth. I then hit him on his buttocks until they went quite red. He did not react in the least. I thought that it was spite that made him want not to show that he felt anything, and I fell into a rage about that. So I then hit him hard in the testicles. At that he finally stretched his arm out to pick something up. It was a monocle that he inserted into one eye without making a sound.

Los Angeles, 26 September 1948

We had been invited to dinner by Sch. The meal took place on a narrow terrace in front of the house. I sat next to him and in my dream I thought: like a woman who had been made his dinner companion. There was an excellent golden brown soup which was said to be borscht, although it was not remotely like it. – There was plenty of stuff for an argument in Sch.'s self-opinionated style. But I forestalled this by complimenting him on the delicious soup. At this he instantly pounced and said, 'Then you could make a donation.' I asked for whose benefit and he said something about sick children. I explained that I did not have the money for a donation of that sort, but since his mother-in-law, K., had made this excellent soup I could make out a cheque to her for five dollars. He accepted this without further ado and I wrote out the cheque. He then took two old yellow teeth out of his mouth and gave them to me 'as a memento'. He dropped them into my soup, together with a third thing, a sort of slimy heap. I was overcome by a wave of nausea, but I do not know whether I dared to stop eating. The dream went on for a long time. But I cannot remember anything more about it. Later, I slept peacefully.

Los Angeles, September 1948

In emigration, I repeatedly dreamt, with variations, that I was at home in Oberrad, even after the Hitler regime had begun. I sat at my mother's desk in the living room, looking out onto the garden. Autumn, overcast with tragic clouds, an unending melancholy, but a pervasive scent over everything. Everywhere, vases with autumn flowers ('Stell auf den Tisch die duftenden Reseden').[26] I was writing in a blue exercise book like the ones from high school. What I was writing was a long treatise on music. It was the 1932 essay 'On the Social Situation of Music', which somehow merged with the *Philosophy of Modern Music*. I knew that I had sent the whole manuscript (of which I had no copy) to a music journal (the Stuttgarter?), where it was accepted for publication, but could not appear

---

[26] 'Place on the table the sweet-smelling mignonettes' – the only verse to have survived from the writings of the Tirolean poet Hermann von Gilm (1812–1864). The poem from which this line was taken was set to music by Richard Strauss.

because of the Nazis, and had then gone missing. The source of anxiety in this dream was the idea that I had to find the manuscript because it contained ideas of the greatest importance for my current project. As I continued writing, the dream and this idea became so powerful that I started to doubt whether that handwritten text had not existed in reality, and it took all my strength to convince myself that it hadn't. Once I had finished the *Philosophy of Modern Music* the dream ceased to recur. Its true meaning is evidently the retrieval of the European life that has been lost. It coincided with Max's travelling to Europe in the spring of 1948.

Los Angeles, 1 October 1948

A ball or party, but I seemed to be on my own on the dance floor. The organizers assigned girls to all the participants, and I was waiting for the girl who had been chosen for me and whom I did not know. She then appeared on a platform and danced towards me. I observed with pleasure that she had beautiful legs – in ochre-coloured stockings – and that she was very pretty. I could see from her clothes, and perhaps also from the shape of her face, that she was a Bulgarian (although her face was perhaps more that of a native of Trieste). She guided me with such skill that, although I am a rotten dancer, I imagined I was dancing well. Nevertheless, I slipped my hand into her dress at the back and gave her bottom a feel. At the same time, I drew her close to me as we danced, and we went on dancing, kissing each other all the time. The ball now seemed to be in full swing. Then a man, perhaps a passing dancer, called out to me in English, in an extremely aggressive tone. He said that the way I was squeezing the girl's behind in public amounted to an act of criminal indecency in America and that it could get me gaoled. Horrified, I let go of the girl, who immediately vanished. I hastily went into an adjacent, dimly lit room where people were eating. A table had been reserved for 'my party', but only Sybil Dreyfuß was sitting there. I joined her, saying that the lady with me would come right away, although I knew that this was not the case.

Los Angeles, 6 December 1948

At 8.20 a.m. I was woken up by our lawyer ringing the doorbell, on account of our eviction. I was in the midst of a dream. We were in a little South German or Hessian town. We parked the car in the main street, and I went into a side street, where I discovered an indescribably beautiful old town hall. I asked a girl who was in conversation with a man about the labour service what the town was called. She professed not to know. When I spoke of the beauty of the square, she pointed mockingly to the large number of visitors, as if to indicate to me that I hadn't exactly made a great discovery. On the way back some people called out erotic remarks to me from a high-lying building. – Change of scene. A couple had been caught making love in the third-class carriage of a train and someone sang them a song whose words and tune occurred in my dream: 'The cutlets are playing a dog's game, a dog's game, a dog's game; the cutlets are playing a dog's game all the livelong day.' Followed by the musical notes. (What was meant was that the dogs were romping and smooching.)

Frankfurt, summer 1952

I was on a committee that was supposed to decide whether the texts of many baroque chorales were so eccentric that they could no longer be sung today. I went into a church with G. in which we could hear music being played. I concentrated on the text and picked up a verse that evidently referred to Jesus and that was being sung to the melody of 'O Haupt voll Blut und Wunden'[27] [O Sacred Head sore wounded]. The text here was 'O komm, mein kleiner Trachäer' [O come my little Trachäer]. I awoke thinking: that goes altogether too far. (Trachodon, Achaean, trochee, Galilean.)

Frankfurt, 24 January 1954

Ferdinand Kramer had apparently turned entirely to painting and had invented a new genre: 'practicable painting'. The essence of this was that you could pull individual painted figures out of the painting – a cow or a hippopotamus. You could then stroke it and feel whether it had a soft fleece or a thick skin. A further variant was the pictures of towns that were developed from architect's plans. These might look like cubist or infantile designs and even remind the observer of Cézanne, tinted pink as in the actual

---

[27] Paul Gerhardt's text, presumably in Bach's setting in the *Matthew Passion*. The following text has no meaning, though, as Adorno indicates, it is rich in associations.

morning sun – I could clearly see such a painting. Benno Reifenberg was said to have published an essay on practicable painting with the title: 'Reconciliation with the Object'.[28]

Frankfurt, January 1954

I heard the unmistakable voice of Hitler coming from loudspeakers with a speech: 'My only daughter fell victim to a tragic accident yesterday. To expiate this, I decree that all trains today will be derailed.' Awoke laughing out loud.

Hamburg, May 1954

Dream during a night in which I thought I could feel my veins swelling and hardening to bursting point. Some kind of disgusting little animals were creating havoc. A toy-size triceratops appeared so as to introduce order, but nothing happened and he finally became indistinguishable from the little animals.

30 July 1954

I dreamt about L. She sat opposite me, looking very elegant, but deathly pale. We embraced like brother and sister. I asked why she looked so awful. 'I am very ill.' 'What's wrong with you then?' 'Cancer.' I tried to talk her out of it.

---

[28] Ferdinand Kramer was an architect and a childhood friend of Adorno's; Benno Reifenberg (1892–1970) was a well-known journalist who worked on the *Frankfurter Zeitung* during the Weimar Republic and sat on the editorial board of its successor, the *Frankfurter Allgemeine Zeitung*, after 1958.

By way of reply she took all her clothes off. Her body, especially in its most private parts, was horrifyingly disfigured; it seemed to be covered with a bluish-red coating. I exerted all my strength to prevent her from seeing me shudder, and we made love. As we did so, I asked her what sort of cancer she had, and she replied: 'Armchair cancer.'

Locarno, 30 August 1954

St Charles Borromeo is said to have tried to enter the man on the cross through the anus. Through a miracle, this had opened to receive him and Borromeo had vanished inside completely. This was why he had been canonized. It was not quite clear whether he had performed this act on the living Jesus or a statue. Nevertheless, I saw clearly how he clambered around on a cross and busied himself between Jesus' legs. By profession Borromeo was said to have been a colonel. I dreamt all this in utter seriousness, which lasted even after I had woken up, when I burst out laughing so much that I had to restrain myself so as not to wake Gretel. This is why the church is known as St Borromäus im Gedärme [St Borromeo in the Guts] or, as the Bavarians say: St Borromäus im Oarsch [St Borromeo in the Arse].

A few days earlier an indescribably ghastly dream that is probably not unconnected with it. I was in a pub on the River Main, the first building in the Old Town you come to after the Alte Brücke. I was not alone (was my mother with me?). The place was full of monstrosities and extremely tiny dwarfs, including a bare negro head; these monstrosities walked around on legs like lobsters, trying to attack people's genitals. In reply to my question I was told that it was a kind of masochist brothel, but it sounded like mockery: we were all to be martyred. I had the same fear as a child has of a disreputable district or, later on, when a nightclub hostess grabbed me through my trousers. Then, in the depths of the night, at the corner of Schöne Aussicht and Schützenstrasse. A large number of silent, shadowy people. Superficially calm: they won't do anything to me. Underneath: even greater fear, fear of their unreality.

Frankfurt, 10 September 1954

I dreamt I had taken part in a theological discussion; Tillich was present. A speaker expounded the distinction between 'equibrium' and 'equilibrium'. The former was inner balance, the latter, outer balance. The effort of proving to him that there is no such thing as equibrium was so great that I woke up in the attempt.

20 March 1955

I was playing the piano on the table top, just as I used to when I was a child. But there was music. I can clearly remember very powerful, vivid chords in E flat major of the kind that I would like to be able to produce. I said to G., 'You see, if you are in good form artistically like me, it makes no difference whether you are playing a piano or an old table top.' – Awake at midday, I discussed the dream with her. She pointed out that it sounded like a parody of one of my own theories. I might easily have produced such a theory for the benefit of my students. She asked me why I made fun of myself in my dreams and, without thinking, I answered: to fend off feelings of paranoia.

1 April 1955

Before the dream proper, there was another rather chaotic dream about especially beautiful old houses in Paris or Vienna. It then made a leap to my father's house at Schöne Aussicht 7, which was evidently supposed to be such a beautiful old house. I was in one of the rooms there one night, with Agathe, who later changed into Gretel. We sat in armchairs waiting in trepidation. Above the door there was a pane of glass that was not quite transparent. Suddenly, electric light shone through. I had the feeling that men, murderers perhaps, were outside. Agathe got up to see what was happening; I remained seated, petrified. When she opened the door I did in fact see some rather intimidating men. Agathe seemed to go straight through them without difficulty, and she went up a small stairway to the side, probably to the toilet. Now Gretel began to upbraid me for my indolence or cowardice. I finally prevailed on myself to stand up and go in search of Agathe. An endless parade of men goose-stepped past me. Somehow I realized that they were all going to a shop where they would be able to buy some coarse shirts at ridiculously low prices in a sale. They meant us no harm. At the same moment I realized: it was a procession of ghosts, and woke up.

16 June 1955

Two giant, black triceratops, as if made of plastic, furious, horrifying animals whom I disliked. While one of them looked on, the other attacked an ankylosaurus in an unspeakably ferocious manner. The ankylosaurus lay

spread out on the ground ('a base animal'). The triceratops used its horns to slit it open at what might be called
the suture where its lower and upper half had
grown together like an edible crab. It then removed the
upper half. The internal organs lay in the lower half
neatly distributed in compartments, each with a different
colour, like a dish of hors d'oeuvres. The triceratops
fell upon it and began to devour the different parts, each of
which represented a different taste (concretism) – once
again just like an edible crab. I was just thinking
indignantly: but the triceratops are vegetarians, when I
woke up.

5 September 1955

Life is myth. Proof: the root βί in βίοζ, vi in vita is identical with μυ.

Stuttgart, September 1955

One night in S. I dreamt that the most agonizing method of
execution – for which I was evidently destined – would be
to stand up to one's head in water while being roasted at the
same time. The dousing qualities of the water would make
it last for an especially long time.

Frankfurt, end of October 1955

I was supposed to take part in a performance of [Schiller's]
Wallenstein – presumably as an actor – not on the stage, but
in a film or television programme. My job was to liaise with
the different actors by telephone; say, with Max Piccolomini,
Questenberg or Isolani. I phoned up and asked for the

young Prince Piccolomini – although it is his father who becomes a prince right at the end, after Max's death. He came to the phone, a character like St Loup,[29] extremely charming and affable. I ask him whether it wouldn't be simpler for him to come over to my boarding house – in Berlin – for lunch. He agreed at once. Highly pleased with myself, I sat down in an armchair, thinking, 'You did that well.' This was immediately followed by the nagging worry that I did not know what to do next.

Frankfurt, 12 November 1955

I dreamt that I had to take the exam for the diploma in sociology. It went badly in empirical sociology. I was asked how many columns there are in a punch card, and, as a pure guess, I said twenty. Of course, that was wrong. The situation was even worse when it came to concepts. I was given a number of English terms and was asked to give their exact meanings in empirical sociology. One term was: *supportive*. I translated like a good boy, giving the German words for supportive, assisting. But it turned out that in statistics it meant the precise opposite, something altogether negative. Taking pity on my ignorance, the examiner then announced that he would question me on cultural history. He showed me a German passport of 1879. It ended with the farewell greeting: 'Now out into the world, my little wolf!' This motto appeared in gold leaf. I was asked to explain this. I took a deep breath and explained that the use of gold for such purposes went back

[29] St Loup is a character in Proust's *À la recherche du temps perdu*.

to Russian or Byzantine icons. The idea of the prohibition on images had been taken very seriously in those parts; only gold had been exempted. Because it was the purest metal, an exception was made for it. Its use in illustrations was followed by baroque ceilings and then by furniture intarsia, and the gold lettering in the passport was to be the last vestige of that great tradition. The examiners were delighted by the profundity of my knowledge and I passed the exam.

28 November 1955

I had a terrible row with my mother, who announced that she was under no obligation to support me materially. I shouted at her: a curse on the body that gave me birth. I transferred to her my anger at the mother of J. (super ego) and at the same time gave expression to my own death wish. NB theatrical pathos.

9 January 1956

I remember a complex. I was in a medium-sized town and drove from the station along a road that seemed very familiar to me. It was a quarter with a large number of restaurants where one could eat well, but where the atmosphere was somewhat louche. In one of these I met a girl on the margins of prostitution. She was dark and I found her very attractive, without actually being beautiful. So I always slept with her. These events seemed so vivid to me that I found it hard to decide whether I had really experienced them. That is precisely the pattern that operates when one is gripped by madness.

24 January 1956

After a day marked by wild hope and deepest depression, I found myself in the open air, beneath an indescribably black sky full of scurrying clouds. It seemed to threaten imminent catastrophe. Suddenly there was a light, like lightning, but yellower and less bright. It came from one particular point and disappeared quickly under or over the clouds, but not as quickly as a flash of lightning. I said that it was a hurricane and someone confirmed this. There followed a long, indescribable roar, more like the reverberation of an explosion than of thunder; apart from that, nothing happened. I asked whether that was all, and that too was confirmed. Still feeling very excited, and at the same time reassured, I awoke. It was the middle of the night; I went back to sleep.

Frankfurt, 18 November 1956

I dreamt of a catastrophic fire. In the cosmic inferno all the dead reappeared in their former shape for a few seconds, and I realized: only now are they truly dead.

Frankfurt, 9 May 1957

At a concert with G., where I heard a great vocal work, probably with a choir. In this a monkey played an outstanding part. I explained to G. that this was the monkey from *Das Lied von der Erde* which had strayed from there and was now making a guest appearance, following the usual practice.

7 June 1957

I dreamt I was in a concentration camp. I heard a group of Jewish children singing a song with the text 'Our good Mamme has not yet been hanged.' (NB J. calls her mother Mamme.)

25 June 1957

Once again I was to be crucified. A group of advisers assisted me. Thassilo von Winterfeldt asked me whether I had ever been crucified before. He explained to me that crucifixion was most unpleasant. I should not fail to take exercise so as to increase my circulation and to prevent cramp and stiffness. While I was trying to explain to him that this was the very purpose of crucifixion, I awoke.

Sils-Maria, 23 August 1957

A concert was due to take place in the main hall of the university. However, it was not the main hall but a faded red music room. Access was difficult since the floor was completely covered with glass splinters. In order to get through, I did the most stupid thing possible: I took my shoes off and walked in my socks. In this way, I managed to move to the front. The vice-chancellor was seated there. He explained to me at length how he had originally worked on romantic jurisprudence. Othmar Spann. I drew his attention to the glass splinters. They had been scattered, I said, by people who had hired the room earlier. As the master of the house and a lawyer, he was in a position to take legal action. He admitted that he had not thought of that, but said that I was completely right. I then looked rather manically, as is my wont, round the room to see whether my girl-friend was present, but couldn't see her. On the other hand, U. lay on a kind of scaffolding, with H. fussing round her. She explained to me immediately with great emphasis that Miss Sch. had asked her to pass on her most affectionate farewell greetings. Even while the dream was still going on, I realized that this was E. and woke up laughing. (A real gift for a psychoanalyst.)

Sils-Maria, 21 August 1958

A museum concert in Frankfurt. Brahms's Violin Concerto was on the programme, but played by Serkin, a pianist. In fact, I recognized the work note by note, and followed it scrupulously. It was evidently a magnificent, virtuoso piano version, one that could only have come from the pen of Brahms himself. Everything was absolutely faithful to the original work, except for a very strange change roughly at the start of the development section which completely broke with Brahms's style. At this point Serkin called out to the audience: 'That is the first gesture', emphasizing the final syllable, perhaps in a Hungarian fashion. He then proceeded in this outlandish way, repeating at every new section: 'This is the second gesture, this is the third gesture.' The audience became restive and gradually started to laugh. Serkin fell into a rage, saying the best thing would be for them all to go home. After this, people did in fact start to leave the hall, first in ones and twos, and then in groups. Only a few avant-gardists, Kolisch[30] among them, clapped demonstratively. Finally, the bearded president of the Museum Society stood up demonstratively with his wife and declared loudly that he was resigning from the chairmanship.

Mid-September 1958

Rest of the day: I had been invited by the headmaster of my high school, which is now called the Freiherr vom Stein-Schule, to contribute something to a *Festschrift* in honour of its fiftieth anniversary. Dream: a ceremony in which I had been solemnly installed as head of music of the high school. The repulsive old music teacher, Herr Weber, together with a new music teacher, danced attendance on me. After that, there was a great celebratory ball. I danced with a giant yellowish-brown Great Dane – as a child such a dog had been of great importance in my life. He walked on his hind legs and wore evening dress. I submitted entirely to the dog and, as a man with no gift for dancing, I had the feeling that I was able to dance for the first time in my life, secure and without inhibition. Occasionally, we kissed, the dog and I. Woke up feeling extremely satisfied.

[30] Rudolf Kolisch (1896–1978) was an avant-garde violinist. He was a great friend of Adorno and the brother-in-law of Schoenberg. He established his own string quartet, with which he pioneered performances of modern music, including works by Schoenberg, Berg and Webern.

28 January 1959

I was in a small, circular room with a very high ceiling. A few people sat in a circle: the most powerful people in the world. It was the crucial meeting about the outbreak of a nuclear war. From time to time, someone would stand up without saying a word and then resume his seat. I thought to myself: a game of poker. They all had bright red faces. Suddenly something that I could not identify revealed that a decision had been taken in favour of war. I awoke thinking that one must pray that something would survive. – A few days later, I saw the sky at night, covered with white signs scurrying across the heavens, watched breathlessly by onlookers. Suddenly, one of them signalled the same decision.

Frankfurt, end of December 1959

Execution dream. Beheading. Not clear if my head was to be chopped off or guillotined. But so as to keep it still, I placed it in a groove. The blade scraped away at my neck, unpleasantly trying it out. I asked the executioner to spare me this and get on with it. The blow fell but I did not wake up. My head was now lying in a ditch, as was I. I waited on tenterhooks to see whether I would go on living or whether after a few seconds all thought would be extinguished. Soon, however, there could be no doubt of my continued existence. I observed that my body was gone, but that I was still there, quite apart from my head. I also seemed capable of perception. But I then discovered to my horror that every avenue through which I might show myself or communicate had been completely cut off. I thought to myself that the nonsensical nature of a belief in spirits was that it suppresses the decisive factor, the very thing that characterizes pure spirit, namely its absolute invisibility [?], and that it thereby betrays spirit to the world of the senses. Whereupon I awoke.

I must have felt a strong desire to urinate while I was still asleep. At all events, I was looking for somewhere to relieve myself, feeling extremely uncomfortable all the while, in fact desperate and full of anxiety that I would be unable to control myself. Then I found a large, white elegant lavatory in a grand hotel, perhaps the St Francis in San Francisco. I was shocked to see that in it preparations were in train for a ladies' party, doubtless for a women's club. Everything had been decorated, rows of chairs had been set out for a concert and the urinals had been festooned with wreaths, flower arrangements and roses. Servants rushed around busily. But nothing could stop me from relieving myself. However, the quantity of urine that flooded out of me turned out to be so vast that the bowl overflowed and flooded the entire banqueting hall. Without any end in sight, I awoke with a feeling of horror.

16 June 1960

The night before I left [for Vienna], I dreamt that the reason why I cannot relinquish all metaphysical hope is not because I cling to life, but because I would like to wake up with G.

Vienna, 26 June 1960

The night before last I dreamt that one day it had remained completely dark. For the first time since the creation of the world, the sun had failed to rise. There had been various explanations; according to one of them the end of the world was nigh, to another an atom bomb had exploded over London and the soot it threw up had spread over the whole world and darkened it. I went outdoors and saw a vast, hilly, immeasurably peaceful landscape. It lay before me as if in the moonlight, although no moon was to be seen. Utterly comforting. The dream was obviously connected with my meeting with Helene Berg.

Frankfurt, 10 October 1960

Kracauer appeared to me. My dear chap, it is a matter of indifference whether we write books and whether they are good or bad. They will be read for a year. Then they will be put in the library. Then the headmaster will come along and distribute them among the kids [*an die Kinner*].

Frankfurt, 13 April 1962

I was due to sit an exam, an oral exam in geography. I was the only person to do this out of a large number of examinees, probably in the entire university. I was told that this was a privilege thanks to my other achievements. I was to be examined by Leu Kaschnitz.[31] My task was to define exactly what area had been occupied by a particular, precisely delimited district in an older description of the city

---

[31] Leu was the nickname of Marie Luise Kaschnitz (1901–1971), a well-known and much respected German writer and poet, friendly with the Adornos after the latter's return to Germany after the war.

of Rome, a grey, soft-cover octavo volume. The tools I was given consisted of a yellow folding ruler, a large and small paper pad, and some pencils. Somewhere or other there was also a map, but one glance told me that it represented not Rome but Paris. An isosceles triangle had been drawn on it, with the Seine as a base and Montmartre as its top. I had the feeling that this triangle was meant to be the district I was measuring. Leu was meant to be invigilating while I carried out this task, but she asked me to get a move on as she was short of time. At first blush, the problem seemed ridiculously easy, as if I had been given something to do that could be accomplished by diligence and meticulous attention to detail, rather than something that might exceed my knowledge and abilities. So I set to work, as rationally as if I had been awake. But I then ran into difficulties. In the first place, it was not clear to me whether I was supposed only to calculate the space occupied by the printed description – which seemed to be indubitably the case when the problem had been set; or whether, as I thought more rational, I was supposed to calculate the size of the district itself. However, in accordance with the maxim that one should stick to the literal statement (perhaps because the alternative possibility seemed too problematic), I opted for the first interpretation. That is to say, I was to use the ruler to measure the height and width of the printed matter and multiply the figures. Given my short-sightedness, I doubted whether I could carry out these measurements with the requisite precision. Moreover, the marked area started in the middle of a line and ended in the middle of another. I would therefore have to measure the tiny extra spaces and subtract them from the total; that seemed the most ticklish bit of the entire enterprise. The brochure's title page contained, beneath the name of the author, which escapes me, the word 'student'. I believed that I was within my rights to discuss this with Leu, even though, once she had set me the task, I could not ask her anything else. 'This was obviously done by some poor student', I said, as if this were of great moment. 'Yes, very touching', said Leu; we were pleased to be in agreement about this. I went on reading, and under the word 'student' I now saw the word 'Old Catholic'. I recollected that the Old Catholics were the group of people who had split off from the Church when Pius IX had proclaimed papal infallibility. The brochure must be an anti-papist tract and the district in question had to be the Vatican. Now I understood the meaning of the map of Paris: it was the Babel of sins. The entire project had an esoteric meaning and it was thought that the task of deciphering it was within my powers: how large is Hell? I revealed to Leu something of my discovery and she seemed delighted by my progress. After this, I set to work with a will. I now found myself in a lofty ruin, perhaps the Baths of Caracalla. Relying on my common sense, I made a rough estimate so as not to go astray in my calculations and to have some idea of the size of the entire area from the outset. While doing this I was interrupted. It turned out that there was a second candidate, a renowned scholar. He was laughing at me, in the first place because the task was so easy, but, secondly, he pointed out that it contained traps for the unwary that I would inevitably fall into. I was not at all disconcerted by this: he didn't really mean me ill, that was just his way, but it did irritate me to the extent that I woke up. It took me quite a time before I realized that the whole thing had been a dream.

Frankfurt, 18 September 1962

I held a copy of the printed version of Benjamin's *Arcades Project* in my hands, though it was not clear whether he had completed it after all or whether I had reconstructed it myself from the drafts. I looked through it lovingly. One title read: 'Part Two' or 'Chapter Two'. Beneath it stood the motto:

> 'What tramcar would be so impertinent
> as to maintain that it only moved for the
> sake of the crunching of the sand?
> > Robert August Lange, 1839'

18 October 1963

I met Jean Cocteau shortly before his death. He had turned into a young girl, an East European Jewess.

Baden-Baden, 25 March 1964

A psychotherapist wished to give a talk on Schubert from the point of view of his own discipline. It was to take place in a very large hotel. The speaker's rostrum had a curtain in front of it and resembled a puppet theatre. Suddenly, the large hall seemed to be like the ones they have in country hotels, such as the Frankfurter Hof in Kronberg. A pub pianist in a shabby evening jacket and a stained shirt with a soft collar began to bang away on a rickety, out-of-tune piano. After a few introductory bars, the psychotherapist launched into a boozy, off-key rendition of 'Ich schnitt es gern in alle Rinden ein'[32] in an exaggerated Viennese dialect, Ottakring dialect to be precise, as if it were the 'Fiakerlied'.[33] He wanted to create the right mood. As in Hollywood, the distinction between Schubert and operetta became blurred. I felt overcome by an insensate fury. I sought out the guests of the hotel, which by now had been transformed back into a grand hotel with innumerable smaller rooms where they all sat around dispersed into little groups. I harangued them with the argument that this performance was so barbaric that it turned anyone who tolerated it into a barbarian as well. My eloquence did not go unheeded. We all joined forces to beat the psychotherapist to death. I became so agitated that I awoke.

Frankfurt, 19 July 1964

I dreamt that Scholem[34] had told me the story of a Old Norse saga. A knight had wooed a girl; there had been difficulties and he had abducted her with the aid of a rope ladder. This saga was said to have formed the basis of the German folksong 'Fuchs, du hast die Gans gestohlen' [Fox, you have stolen the goose].

[32] I.e. 'I would like to carve it on every tree-trunk', from 'Ungeduld' [Impatience], from Schubert's *Die schöne Müllerin*.
[33] A popular Viennese cab-driver's song.
[34] Gershom Scholem (1897–1982), the celebrated philosopher and expert on Jewish studies, friendly with Walter Benjamin and also Adorno.

Sils-Maria, 4 September 1964

(Shortly before waking up)

I had to write a six-hour-long school essay on Goethe. I realized at once that I had to fix on a complex of central importance. For this reason I launched into an interpretation of 'So laß mich scheinen, bis ich werde'.[35] My thesis went: Goethe endowed the language with so much earth that its gravity sank and released its content. I went to endless trouble to elaborate this idea. The mere writing down of each word cost me a huge effort and seemed to last an eternity. During this work I was in a panic about whether I could complete the task in the time available to me, and whether any teacher would be able to understand the essay, so that I would end up with a bad mark. I was in such a panic that I woke up.

22 December 1964

Invitation to Consul Schubert, not in his magnificent villa, but in a more modest flat occupying an entire floor, much like that of my Uncle Louis on the Eschersheimer Landstrasse. Guest of honour: Kaiser Wilhelm, who made a very unpretentious entrance, an old man but with the kind of beard fashionable before 1914, his moustache and hair dyed black. His wife, also very old, was Else Herzberger.[36]

[35] 'So let me seem till I become' – Mignon's poem in *Wilhelm Meisters Lehrjahre*. A key poem for Adorno; see Afterword, p. 105.
[36] Else Herzberger was a close friend of Adorno. His father's wine merchant's business had links with the firm of Karplus and Herzberger, who were in the tanning business. Adorno met his

She greeted me very naturally and with great warmth: 'There you are, my boy, everything will be just the way it used to be.' The Kaiser sat down on a sofa. He began to stick high-denomination banknotes between his feet and his toes. Using his feet, he distributed tips to the numerous servants who were present. This was explained by the statement that no one could expect him to touch their hands with his. Hardly anything could be seen of the other people present.

Frankfurt, December 1964

The world was about to end. At the crack of dawn, with the sky still grey and not yet really light, I found myself in a large crowd on a kind of ramp, with hills on the horizon. Everyone stared at the sky. Still half dreaming, I asked whether the world would *really* come to an end now. People confirmed that it was so, talking just as people talk who are technically in the know; they were all experts. In the sky three huge, menacing stars could be seen; they formed an isosceles triangle. They were due to collide with the earth shortly after 11 a.m. Then a loudspeaker announced that at 8.20 a.m. Werner Heisenberg would speak once again. I thought that that couldn't be him acting as commentator on the end of the world. It could only be the repetition of a tape recording that had often been played. I awoke with the feeling that, if the world really were to come to an end, this is how it would happen.

---

wife Gretel Karplus through this connection. In later years, Else was able to help Walter Benjamin when he was in financial difficulties in exile in Paris.

Frankfurt, July 1965

My doctor had lanced a number of boils. I dreamt that, on his bill, he had given them all names. I remember one of them: 'The foul-smelling boil "Étude" '.

Frankfurt, July 1965

Kolisch asked me to accompany him to the execution in the electric chair of someone he knew. I was to be there as a mark of honour for the delinquent, and also as a kind of protest. Our names were then entered in a list of the man's friends. Apart from us, L. N. came too. The execution was held in a radio station, in two rooms, the recording studio and the listening studio, where one could watch through a window. Up there we could see P. S., who was fully in the picture. The condemned man was young and was dressed in a shirt, braces and trousers. He might well have been a student. We spoke a few words and then he was led into the execution chamber. P. S. was unhappy about the delay. A number of pretty children were playing on the floor, scrabbling around menacingly. They were the condemned man's nephews. The chair was like an ordinary barber's chair. He was tied down on it and the current was switched on. It took some time to build up. When it was fully functioning, a fiery cloud formed round the man's head. It spread out over his entire body, and while that was happening I heard a murmuring or singing that seemed to emanate from him. By the time the fire died down, he was singing at the top of his voice. He had been burned right down to the skeleton, which continued to glow. To my unspeakable horror, he got up and, still singing, was led into my listening studio. I recoiled, desperate to avoid all contact. Someone, probably P., explained that there was nothing unusual about this; condemned men often survived another week in this state. Woke up, horrified.

Frankfurt, 22 March 1966

I dreamt that Peter Suhrkamp had written a great book of cultural criticism – in Low German. Its title was *Pa Sürkups sin Kultur* [Pop Suhrkamp, his culture]. (Pa = Peter and Papa; Sürkup = Suhrkamp and the French Admiral Surcouf; sin = his [German: *sein*] and latin *sine*.)[37]

March 1966

I was asked to leave a faculty meeting because they were going to talk about me. When I returned, one of my colleagues, Herr Keller or Herr Patzer, I couldn't make out which, stuck his leg out to trip me up. I complained volubly about this outrageous behaviour. I was told that I did not understand the situation. This was an ancient tradition. What I now had to do was to apply to the dean and make a formal complaint. He would then inform me that the faculty had resolved that I should no longer be permitted to attend its meetings. Overcome with the shock, I awoke.

---

[37] Peter Suhrkamp (1891–1959) founded the Suhrkamp publishing house in 1950. Under Suhrkamp and his successor Siegfried Unseld, it had an immeasurable influence on the publishing and intellectual world in Germany after 1945. Adorno's works were published by Suhrkamp Verlag. Low German is the dialect of German (still) spoken in the north of the country. Robert Surcouf was a French corsair at the time of the Napoleonic wars.

Rome, October 1966

In Rome with Gretel, in a beautiful, large hotel room. I noticed with a shock that in the nearby house opposite us, in a triangular gable, countless people had assembled, a mixture of riff-raff and monstrosities, figures with bald heads and tentacles, such as I had once dreamt of seeing lying around on the ground in a threatening manner. They stared menacingly at us and I then discovered that they were also suspended, like bunches of grapes, immediately under our window, ready to fall upon us. I awoke with an unspeakable sense of horror. (The motif here may be the formation of a Chinese wing among the Italian communists.)

Frankfurt, February 1967

I wanted to obtain my doctorate in law and had thought of a topic that seemed suited to me. It was: the transition from the living human being to the juridical person. I had also formed some ideas about method. As far as possible, it was to be in tune with official scientific principles. My idea was to collect all the definitions of the juridical person discoverable in the literature, explore the differences between them and the living human being, and from there to construct the transition.

March 1967

Dreams of dead people in which you have the feeling that they are asking you for help. The dream of the big party in which Hermann Grab, who was already terminally ill, appeared in a light-blue suit.

14 April 1967

A. said to me: 'I am now thirty years old, but I look twenty-eight years younger.'

Crans, 12 August 1967

I dreamt I was with my eighty-seven-year-old mother. She was in pretty good shape, mentally as well, only boundlessly stubborn. She wanted at all costs to go with me to a resort on the Baltic so as to go swimming. I tried to tell her how risky that was at her age, she could easily catch pneumonia. She just laughed and said categorically: 'Nothing will protect me against the black sickness, I am prone to it.'

27 November 1967

I felt very unwell. Woke up with a proverb that seemed very profound at the time: 'Only when the dogs are fierce will the inhabitants be loyal.'

17 December 1967

I had an indescribably beautiful and elegant mistress; she reminded me of A., but had something of the grande dame about her. I was extremely proud of her. She told me that I absolutely had to acquire a prick-washing machine. I pointed out that I took a bath every day and that I kept myself scrupulously clean. She replied that only such a machine could guarantee that one would be free of every objectionable odour in the relevant place. Only if I were to buy one would she make love to me with her mouth. I was uncertain whether she might not be a saleswoman for the firm that manufactured the machine. Woke up laughing.

The moon was about to crash to earth. I saw it standing pale in the sky during the day, just as it really does appear by day, but about ten times as big. I comforted myself with the optimistic thought that, if it really is made of dust or some other loose substance, the impact will not be so severe.

Munich, 28 October 1968

At the entrance to a concert I encountered Steuermann.[38] I was overjoyed, but also amazed, since I knew he was dead. He wore a very modest brown suit. Of course, I couldn't ask him whether he was still alive, but I expressed the idea through my gestures and he replied in the affirmative, also by gestures. Then he added, 'But my material existence is undermined.' And then, with the self-irony so typical of him, he said, 'The fact is that I have noble passions.' In answer to my question which passions, he said that he never omitted to include precious heraldic symbols in gold and silver in his musical compositions and these had to be printed as components of the music. This passion was destroying him. (In the afternoons, evidently in connection with the death of Josef Gielen and with Ruscha's[39] being left on her own. New musical notation?)

[38] Eduard Steuermann (1892–1964), Polish pianist and a close friend of Adorno, who had met him in Vienna in the 1920s. He had dedicated himself to the cause of modern music, especially that of Schoenberg.

[39] Josef Gielen (1890–1968) was an actor and director in Vienna. After his return from exile during the Nazi period, he played a major role in reviving Austrian theatrical life, both in the

Recklinghausen, 16 March 1969

A. came to my bed in the depths of the night. I asked her: 'Do you love me?' She answered as naturally as if it had been true: 'Madly.' – Sometime later, she was visiting us together with Rudolf Hirsch.[40] The conversation turned to subtlety in Hofmannsthal. A. said something outlandish, whereupon Rudolf moved to sit next to Gretel. – Woken up very early by a bird whose song sounded to me like 'Zwatscha'.

29 March 1969

I dreamt I had received a letter from A. – after two months' silence. I began by eagerly reading the signature. It said: 'For the last time, for the time being. Yours, A.'

Baden-Baden, 11 April 1969

I was walking across a street in a very large town in the middle of the night, perhaps the Kurfürstendamm. Above the entrance to a cabaret the word LULU was written in large letters. I thought it must refer to a possibly shortened version of the opera and went in. I then noticed that there was nothing but a somewhat charmless, down-at-heel striptease dancer, who was trying after a fashion to represent Lulu through her dancing. Repelled, I left the place and woke up with a feeling of shock.

Burgtheater and the Viennese Opera, as well as at the Salzburg festival. Ruscha was his wife Rosa, a sister of Eduard Steuermann.

[40] Rudolf Hirsch (1905–1996) spent the period after 1933 in exile in Holland. From 1950 he became literary editor of the *Neue Rundschau* and also for Fischer Verlag.

Baden-Baden, 12 April 1969

I discussed with A. the plan that we should take our own lives together. In my memory it seems to me that the idea had first come from her; at any rate, she took to it with enthusiasm, in keeping with her customary boldness. We considered whether we should jump from a high tower like R. P., but decided against it. Finally, she said: 'In that case I shall try to die together with you.' The word 'try' made me feel that she did not really mean it. Awoke with a feeling of disappointment that grew into abhorrence. – Later the same night. Apparently on the basis of his psychoanalytical experience, Habermas said to me that it was very dangerous to surrender inwardly to whatever moved me; that could easily lead to the development of cancer.

— Afterword —

Think of how puzzling a dream is. Such a
riddle doesn't *have* to have a solution. It
intrigues us. It is *as if* there were a riddle
here.[1]
Why should dreaming be more
mysterious than the table? Why should
they not both be equally mysterious?[2]

Ludwig Wittgenstein

I

What we know is that Adorno wished to publish a
volume containing the record of his own dreams. As far
back as 1942, he had published some in *Der Aufbau* with
the title 'Träume in Amerika. Drei Protokolle' [Dreams
in America: Three Notes]. These are the dreams that
appear here dated 30 December 1940, 22 May 1941 and
January 1942. These dreams were published by Rolf
Tiedemann in Volume 20.2 of the *Gesammelte Schriften*,
together with a further sixteen that Adorno had selected
for publication in 1968 but which did not in fact appear.
The sheaf of typewritten notes is now published for the
first time in the present volume. As far as we know, these
typescripts came into being in the following way:
Adorno wrote down his dreams 'on waking up'; fair
copies were then made by his wife, Gretel Adorno, and
Adorno himself then made a few changes or added some
explanatory notes, but only in exceptional cases. The

printed version follows the typescripts without further alterations.

We know in addition that some dreams have found their way into other books. Thus the notes on the dream of 16 April 1943 were incorporated into *Minima Moralia* under the title of Monograms.[3] Such use suggests that Adorno regarded the dream notes as raw material for other sorts of text, or at least as the preliminary stage for more fully shaped versions of his dreams along the lines of those we encounter in Wieland Herzfelde,[4] Ernst Jünger[5] or Franz Fühmann.[6] The dream texts of these writers are 'attempts to treat the dream as a literary form',[7] as Fühmann has put it, and the reader can see this even if he is unaware of the different stages the text has undergone.[8] We cannot exclude the possibility that Adorno may have wished to treat individual dreams in a similar way. But even if he did, it is clear that he intended to publish the majority as a book with the dreams in their original or lightly edited form. The dreams contained in the *Gesammelte Schriften* are preceded by the following note by Adorno which refers specifically to the selection published by Rolf Tiedemann:

> These Dream Notes, which have been chosen from a much larger collection, are authentic. I wrote them all down immediately on waking and in preparing them for publication have only corrected obvious linguistic lapses.
>
> T.W.A.

Nor is there any indication that Adorno had intended to supplement the dreams in the proposed volume by adding a commentary or theoretical interpretation of any kind.

We may assume that what Adorno planned was simply a collection of dreams and that the volume would have looked much like the present publication.

However, he would surely have added an introduction, although it would be pointless to speculate what it might have contained. It would be equally futile to make conjectures about the meaning that Adorno might have given to a volume of 'Dream Notes' in the context of his oeuvre as a whole. There is simply not enough clear evidence to go on. Hence in agreeing to the publisher's request to write an afterword to this volume, I decided not to concern myself with such matters and intend only to explain how *I* read the book. Anyone who is not interested in my reading may safely skip what follows.

II

That one should avoid recounting one's dreams in the morning on an empty stomach is a much-quoted warning from Walter Benjamin's *One-Way Street*. Benjamin himself calls this a 'popular tradition' and interprets it as follows:

> Though awake, one remains under the spell of the dream. . . . He who shuns contact with the day, whether for fear of his fellow men or for the sake of inward composure, is unwilling to eat and disdains his breakfast. He thus avoids a rupture between the nocturnal and the daytime worlds – a precaution justified only by the combustion of dream in a concentrated morning's work, if not in prayer; otherwise this avoidance can be a source of confusion between vital rhythms. In this condition, the narration of dreams can bring calamity, because a person

still half in league with the dream world betrays it
in his words and must incur its revenge. To express
this in more modern terms: he betrays himself.[9]

Benjamin's explanation is compatible with both of the for-
mulae which are used to introduce the telling of a dream:
'a dream came to me' [*mir hat geträumt*] and 'I dreamed'
[*ich habe geträumt*]. In the first case, I would be disclosing
something alien to me that has turned me into the theatre
of its own presence; in the second, I would disclose myself,
i.e. also something alien of which *a priori* I know only that
it is myself.

Benjamin goes on to say, 'He has outgrown the protection
of dreaming naïveté, and in laying hands on his dream
visages without thinking, he surrenders himself. For only
from the far bank, from broad daylight, may a dream be
addressed from the superior vantage of memory. . . . The
fasting man tells his dream as if he were talking in his sleep.'[10]

These statements may lead on to all kinds of suggestive
insights, but in the first instance they are no more than a
hermeneutic guideline. They are followed in Benjamin's
text by the narration of three dreams. These dreams, so we
must conclude from the preceding warning, were not
dreamt *precisely in this way*. More precisely, they were not
written down directly on waking up (before breakfast), or,
if they were, the decision to let them stand as they were was
taken from the opposite shore, from the state of complete
wakefulness and, above all, this decision was one we have
not been told about.

If we pause to reflect on the matter a little we begin
to feel a certain dissatisfaction, and this leads to the

question: What's the point of all this? What's the point of such introductory words as: 'In a night of despair, I dreamed . . .' or 'In a dream I saw myself . . .'[11] if they do not point to the raw material of the dream but only to a reworking with an eye to the concerns of the waking day? How do I know that this reworking is not just there to persuade me that the writer is able to dream what another person could not dream of inventing for himself? Or that he has not withheld the best part from me? On the other hand, we may object that even in the best case I never have more than a story. As mere raw material, a dream occurs only to the dreamer and then only in a dream. As he awakens, the dream is worked on by memory, noted down in language, subsequently changed . . . The very statement that a dream occurs in its pure form only in a dream is at bottom no more than a seductive metaphor that acts as if dreams had a substantial reality that manifested itself in dreams, as if one were doing more than just dreaming. But do we not dream the same dream several times over? And is it the same dream or are they just similar? And similar to what, if not to the way in which we talk about them so as to prove that they are just repetitions?

A person who tells his dream, and – whether or not he begins with 'A dream came to me' or 'I had a dream' or 'I dreamt I saw . . .' – says that he is doing so, claims to impart something which he has not consciously shaped or influenced, something that has not been subjected to the control of a supposedly substantive or functional self. He may well mean much more by it and even believe that he is saying much more, but that much at least he is saying; otherwise, he could, indeed he ought to, leave it unsaid. When he adds that the dream narrative is not 'uttered as if he were still asleep' but after breakfast, no longer on an empty stomach and now in full possession of his senses, he informs us that he is telling us only what he wishes to tell us in his present condition, that he is not speaking out of turn or betraying himself, but – well, what then? That he is revealing a secret after all? It is true enough that dreams need not appear mysterious to us. However, when we are told of them, they do seem to be so. This is the only respect in which, however polished they become in the telling, we obtain a glimpse of their true status as material. Moreover, they are to be adjudged material from a formal point of view.

It is easy to become entangled in paradoxes here and to start talking about 'the form of the unformed'. We may do this, but it leads nowhere. A text must display certain characteristics if we are to accept it as the communication of a dream. They include at the very least a lack of plausibility and also a certain pointlessness. A lack of plausibility: we know that dreams flout the rule that changes of scene must be motivated and that we have to know why people appear on the scene or leave it. We expect dream narratives to fail to provide the relevant plausible explanations. If they did provide them we would feel dissatisfaction and refuse to call the story a dream. Conversely, we often compare stories with dreams if we are not told enough about why the people in them act as they do. The point at issue here is not the improbable or the unusual. Any story may contain examples of that; it is necessary only to make clear why they are there. A story has only to be introduced with the words 'Once upon a time' for us to be mentally prepared for more or less anything, even for quite unmotivated actions, actions that 'just happen'. Alternatively, the story can be called 'Sintram and his Companions', can be written by Friedrich de la Motte Fouqué and be too long for a dream – and then we call it 'Romanticism', adding perhaps that it contains 'dreamlike elements'.[12] In other words, if such stories lack something that dream narratives also lack, we make use of some genre description or other to explain why we should not be irritated by the story. Of course, the same thing may hold good for a dream. We only have to read 'In a dream I saw . . .' for everything to become clear. This explains why we need to add the criterion of pointlessness. What is meant by this is the impression that the extravagant occurrence of strange events in a dream has somehow been wasted. It is not just that the jokes that make us laugh in dreams or as we wake up all seem at best only moderately funny by the light of day, or that the majority of dreams peter out, have no proper ending and just come to a stop, but that even when they do possess something like a conventional point it somehow has a botched effect.

In his essay on Kafka, Benjamin tells the story of the clerk Shuvalkin who manages to extract from his depressed master Potemkin the signatures to official documents that have been piling up during the latter's illness, only to discover that, in the darkness of his sick room, the latter has written not 'Potemkin' but 'Shuvalkin' over and over again. This story evidently has a point, albeit one that is open to different interpretations. The story is designed to culminate in this point; the tension in it (urgent need for the signatures, Potemkin's unavailability, Shuvalkin's elation, the futility of his efforts) is fully resolved. The position is different with Benjamin's dream of visiting Goethe's house:

> It was a perspective of whitewashed corridors like those in a school. Two elderly English lady visitors and a curator are the dream's extras. The curator requests us to sign the visitors' book lying open on a desk at the farthest end of a passage. On reaching it, I find as I turn the pages my name already entered in big, unruly, childish characters.[13]

This is a mysterious moment, and we can see that it is a dream story from the way it emerges from some erratic source rather than constituting a point. If we continued the text in a plausible way: '. . . and I remembered suddenly that as a child I had been there once before, but had forgotten . . .', this would have been unspeakably crass, but, even more significantly, it would have sacrificed most of its dreamlike quality. Another possibility would have been to omit the two English ladies and to continue the story with the words: 'I signed my name a second time, but was shocked to discover that my handwriting had become the scarcely legible script of an old man. I realized that I was now dead and awoke with a scream.' Such an ending would feel manipulative. That is how it feels when dream narratives are inserted into other stories and the fictional characters gradually discover their meaning in the course of the main narrative. A point like the one just invented is both too significant and too obvious to be a genuine dream: too significant because we have an intuitive grasp of dream logic that at least tells us that it does not conform to the conventions of fiction; too obvious because it blatantly signals 'deeper meaning', and to distort a dream in this way would be to rob it of something essential.

But this 'essential something' can only be defined as the absence of something, and this may justify our speaking of dreams as 'material' and 'formless', even though we encounter them as something formed, namely as dream narratives. Form, however, and this is something Adorno always insisted on, is internalized social coercion. If you have heard young children telling jokes and stories about their experiences, and seen what a mess they make of it, you will have vividly experienced this coercion in the shape of your own feeling of impatience. Children get lost in a mass of details which consist of the things that were and are important to the child, instead of the information that makes the story interesting, and the story then reaches its climax with a statement like '. . . and then we arrived and I got an ice-cream', or something of the sort. And everyone is supposed to think the story is wonderful because the ice-cream tasted wonderful. This then is unformed material. But adults can change the subject and tell each other stories that they all find interesting even if they are not too interested in each other's well-being, and this is because the stories have a shape: 'and then after all these difficulties we finally succeed in getting there at the last minute, and what do we see but a big sign, saying "Closed on Mondays"', or something of the sort: everyone laughs. Or think of the irritation we feel with someone who cannot organize his material. Such a person seems unable to tell a story in a purposeful manner; instead everything seems two-dimensional so that after five minutes you still have no idea what the important point is. A person like that is regarded as unfocused or even stupid – or perhaps just insufficiently thoughtful? At any rate, he seems to expect his listeners to pay equal attention to every detail, and that is to ask too much. An effort of that kind is reserved for story-telling in a particular situation, namely that of the kind of 'measured' attention expected of a psychoanalyst during a consultation. This kind of attentiveness is also appropriate for listening to dream narratives, but to expect it in ordinary communication would be excessive. For its part, literature is bound to the normative structures of social communication even if it negates them or sets out to present alternative projects.

Thus, if in its unformed state a dream represents something *not yet* formed, it follows that it can represent something that is authentic because it is original and natural. It may even be a source of the renewal of art from within a sphere inaccessible to societal coercion. However, this is an idea to which Benjamin reacted sceptically. In his essay 'Surrealism' he refers to the programmatic anecdote according to which Saint-Pol-Roux, 'retiring to bed about daybreak, fixed a notice on his door: "Poet at work".' For Benjamin, dreams are just one way of 'loosen[ing] individuality like a bad tooth',[14] but the aim of such an exercise is not to peer into a pre-societal collectivity and its store of images. The aim, rather, is to perceive the ensemble of ordered things as if it had been assembled by the non-form of the dream *ad libitum libidinis*. Benjamin speaks of 'surrealist experiences' for which dream and intoxication could at best provide 'an introductory lesson'. Dreams are not literature per se; literature is not to be found in a diffuse interior that is archaically labelled 'original', but 'at a distance of two metres from the body'. Those who imagine that poets work in their sleep have not 'stumbled upon one of the secrets of poetry', but 'have done away with poetic composition'.[15]

'That is not the way people dream; no one dreams that way', declared Adorno, of the dreams that the surrealists had turned into literature.

> Surrealist constructions are merely analogous to dreams, not more. They suspend the customary logic and the rules of the game of empirical evidence. . . . There is a shattering and a regrouping, but no dissolution. The dream, to be sure, does the same thing, but in the dream the object world appears in a form incomparably more disguised and is presented less as a reality than it is in Surrealism, where art batters its own foundations. The subject, which is at work much more openly and uninhibitedly in Surrealism than in the dream, directs its energy towards its own self-annihilation, something that requires no energy in the dream; but because of that everything becomes more objective, so to speak, than in the dream, where the subject, absent from the start, colours and permeates everything that happens from the wings.[16]

The dream is no subject. Nor does it find itself in the service of subjectivity, it *is* subjectivity. The artist works as subject at the transformation of the objective. Anyone who rearranges existing reality, creates something. Methodically, if he acts methodically. But even if he hands over responsibility for his rearrangement to chance, he still does so as a creator who practises renunciation. The attack on artistic subjectivity is really aimed only at the forms in which artistic subjectivity expresses itself. Even an artist who 'disappears behind objective reality' still objectifies himself as an artist. In dreams everything is subjectivity, there is no countervailing object. It is for this reason that dreams are unconcerned about the quality of their jokes. They do not wish to make good jokes because they do not wish to make anything at all. Dreams lack intentionality because they are themselves intentionality,[17] and this explains why dreams can neither succeed nor fail. Adorno's interest in literary matters developed quite late on, but once it emerged it was sustained; it turned out to be highly selective but was also systematic. We might speculate, despite our good intentions, that this involvement with literature began at a particular point in time with decisive implications for the development of his thought.[18] It is the intellectual conclusion of the *Dialectic of Enlightenment*. As is well known, the theme of that book is the self-destruction of civilization. The process of modernization and rationalization is said to advance the emancipation of mankind from the self-imposed shackles of the mythical interpretation of the world, chiefly through the progressive technological domination of nature. However, this emancipation will succeed only at the cost of a comparable increase in self-control. By replacing the ordering power of myth with the categorizing power of reason, the mythical fear of the unfamiliar will be transformed into the fear of whatever has not yet been subjugated by reason. In this way, the progress of civilization will entail the return of archaic fears and violence: the emancipation from nature leads only to an even more inescapable enslavement by human nature. The hermetic nature of this diagnosis can be seen from the fact that it does not point to any way out from this dilemma: self-knowledge does not lead to a different path since the intellectual tools necessary for the analysis of the civilizing process are themselves an integral part of the dilemma. This notwithstanding, Adorno's philosophy, culminating in *Negative Dialectics*, continues to explore the question (and a possible solution to it) of whether, by insisting on this gesture of futility, it might be possible after all to discover a way of transcending it. This leads Adorno into the linguistic manoeuvres of *Negative Dialectics*, themselves rehearsed in the briefer forms of *Minima Moralia*, in which again and again one sentence controverts another as untrue only to be convicted by the very next sentence as itself implicated in untruth. Adorno's question to literature was about whether it was subject to the same fate. His answer, somewhat surprisingly, was in the negative – albeit a doubly ambivalent negative. On the one hand, he argued, literature was ruled by its own formal laws and was thus spared the necessity of conforming to the laws of social communication. On the other hand, however, these forms involved being coerced into conventions of their own, and this meant that the social order imposed itself in literature too. In line with this, literature must constantly be reminded of its ability to turn towards the avant-garde, whose task is to 'introduce chaos into order rather than the reverse'.[19] Through its struggle with the forms available to it, literature is able to express things that would be mangled if they were expressed directly – the fate of philosophical thought under the yoke of classification. Ideas such as these occasionally border on the meditative and they lead Adorno to a variety of paradoxes and sometimes dilemmas, as can be seen in some of the circular reflections in the *Aesthetic Theory*, though this need not concern us here. But what we should emphasize is that Adorno formulates something like the vision of an ultimate goal for literature that will always enable it to preserve its independence from the pressures to conform that emanate from the processes of communicative societalization. This goal is its ability to say the unsayable. Whatever that may mean. Adorno gives only relatively vague pointers or else would-be authoritative gestures in the direction of a concrete meaning. Where these are sufficiently suggestive, we may wish to hear what he decrees. At bottom, he believes that literature is fully realized only where it abandons its own spirit and becomes music. For, as he argues in his lecture 'On the Classicism of Goethe's *Iphigenie*', insofar as all language is an instrument for the ordering of reality, it is 'involved in enlightenment'.[20] But where language ceases to be able to perform this task, where it loses faith, we might say, in its own contribution to civilization and drifts away from it, it turns into the language of those without concepts, the mute. And whether it does this in Goethe, in Stefan George or in Paul Celan, Adorno believes that there is a further language 'beneath the helpless language of human beings'.[21] This may be no more than the invocation of what doesn't work and can't work, of what cannot be said except in a way that enables emotions rather than thoughts to manifest themselves, seeking out a place in the text and finding it between the lines in accordance with the maxim that 'Only thoughts which do not understand themselves' are 'true'.[22] But even so, these emotions contain a basic motif of Adorno's thought. It is the idea that what really counts, what all intellectual endeavour must concern itself with, is the very thing that ultimately remains inaccessible to it, namely what cannot be reflected upon, what in psychological terms can be called distance from the self, the non-human. This 'non-human reality' may be said to 'reveal' itself in the beauty of nature and sometimes in art:

> The dignity of nature is that of the not-yet-existing; by its expression it repels intentional humanization. This dignity has been transformed into the hermetic character of art, into – as Hölderlin taught – art's renunciation of any usefulness whatever, even if it were sublimated by the addition of human meaning. For communication is the adaptation of spirit to utility. . . . What in artworks is structured, gapless, resting in itself is an afterimage of the silence that is the single medium through which nature speaks.[23]

The only thing that is human in an emphatic sense, according to Adorno, is that which draws closer to the non-human: 'So the expression called human is precisely that of the eyes closest to those of the animal, the creaturely one, remote from the reflection of the self.'[24] This even defines the goal of philosophy: '[Philosophy] exists above all to redeem what lies in the gaze of an animal.'[25]

Not in this way, but in their own way, dreams too are non-intentional. They are intention and realization in one, subject without object, and hence not subject either. As such, they create their own world, but since they exercise no control over the world, but are themselves a world and an order of things that makes no communicative claims, they lack reflective powers, insofar as that is at all possible for mental constructs that can be confronted with the contents of consciousness. It is in this fact that their significance lies. In the 'Lectures on Negative Dialectics' Adorno writes that the 'non-conceptual nature of dreams is combined with their essential importance [*Wesentlichkeit*] for the concept.'[26] It follows that a more appropriate way of preserving them would be to note them down before breakfast.

In my view, the best dream in this collection expresses the non-conceptuality essential for the concept with great virtuosity – I mean the dream dated mid-September 1958, in which the 'I' in the dream finds himself at a celebration in honour of his being appointed head of music in his old high school. He dances 'with a giant yellowish-brown Great Dane' he had known in his childhood and who walks on his hind legs and wears evening dress: 'I submitted entirely to the dog and, as a man with no gift for dancing, I had the feeling that I was able to dance for the first time in my life, secure and without inhibition. Occasionally, we kissed, the dog and I.' Things that cannot be said, things that cannot actually even be thought, can still occur in a dream, and, once there, can even be danced. Adorno whirling around the dance floor and fondly embracing a Great Dane in a dinner jacket is as far as can possibly be imagined from the gravitas of any imageless process of reflection, even though he is at the same time the head of the music department in his Gymnasium. This shows that an idea that is anything but self-evident and that perhaps does not even understand itself may yet be at ease with itself. It shows furthermore that we should consider not merely whether thoughts are consistent or cogent in some other sense, but whether they are charming.

The reader may well be surprised by my unceremonious insistence that a dream is the metaphorical correlative of ideas that the dreamer has allowed to appear in published form. To do this, he will object, is to flout the rules of interpretation. But what kind of interpretation is appropriate here? Psychoanalysis is what people think of first, whatever they think it involves. But psychoanalysis would be quite inappropriate here, if only because of the nature of its own procedures. The psychoanalytic interpretation of a dream is essentially a dialogical process between two people in which what matters crucially are the associations in the mind of the dreamer. It is these associations alone that make it possible to situate the dream experience in the dreamer's life, and this process of situating the dream biographically is essentially the interpretation of the dream. In other words, outside the analytical situation psychoanalysis is just one branch of knowledge among others, one that puts dream and reality together by analogy with interpretations already made. The layman's fear that if he tells the analyst what he has been dreaming he will have bared his soul to someone who knows nothing about him is pure shamanism.[27] Needless to say, we can think of all sorts of things to say about some dreams, and we imagine even more if we have read Freud's *Interpretation of Dreams* and other relevant literature on the topic than if we haven't. It goes without saying that after reading such books people who have dreams about cars and trains will automatically react to the ambiguity of the word 'Verkehr' [which means both 'traffic' and 'intercourse'; Trans.]. And the highly tautological structure of the Babamüll dream (Another night, p. 14), which reveals an artistry of its own, will bring a grin to the face of the reader, even though he knows that the analysis of such a dream in a psychoanalytical setting (and with the active participation of the dreamer) could never be anticipated by a textual analysis. It would be foolish to assume that Adorno did not know what a schematic Freudian (i.e. someone who flouts the rules of psychoanalysis) would make of this or that dream in this collection (and not only of dreams arising from the need to urinate à la 'Little Nemo').[28] Whatever might be 'revealed' by these dreams probably seemed so banal to him as to be worthy of the labour neither of investigation nor of concealment.

People who interpret dreams, by whatever criteria, are dealing with a discourse that is not directed at them, and that is not even a discourse properly speaking, or even a way of talking to oneself. In a psychoanalytical setting a dream becomes a communicative act – because it is communicated to the analyst – and it becomes one in an ambience that supplies an interpretative context. Nothing would be more senseless (and more opposed to the spirit of analysis) than to infer from this preformation that dreams are per se 'nothing but . . .'. Psychoanalytical interpretation is reductive, like interpretation of every kind. There can be no objection in itself to a reductive interpretation. An objection would only be valid if the interpretation were blind to its own reductiveness and claimed an exclusive validity with the formula 'it means nothing but . . .'. Hence the interpretation given above of the dream with the Great Dane should be seen as only one of many possible interpretations in the context of the intellectual architecture of the dreamer's philosophical writings.

Nevertheless, this interpretation does contain a recommendation. Inserted into the context of Adorno's writings as one book among others, the repeated reading of the *Dream Notes* does invest them with a special charm. In the dream of October 1944 the city of Magdeburg appears to have been less badly damaged than Frankfurt. We may 'otherwise' interpret this 'fact' as we want, but the reality is that it belongs in the same context as the section 'Out of the firing-line' in *Minima Moralia*, where a comparison is drawn between the Thirty Years' War and the Second World War. To say this may appear to over-intellectualize images that derive from other sources. In the same way, even if we refrain from interpreting the steeple in standard Freudian terms and from linking it to the first syllable of Magdeburg,[29] some may insist that in terms of logic no act of reasoning is taking place and that it is therefore a mistake to talk about dreams in the same breath as about reasoned arguments that have been committed to paper. However, we may respond to such arguments by pointing out that even the remains left over from the day are never merely the occasion for symbols and puns, and that such a separation of reason and instinct gives neither to reason nor to instinct what properly belongs to either. To assign reason and consciousness to the realm of thought while relegating the unconscious and the irrational to the world of dream is fundamentally misconceived. After all, thinking itself is not something we think; wherever it is that thoughts come from is not a place where our thinking takes place. And only someone who has not thought in his dreams or noticed that he has had thoughts will believe that thinking does not happen in dreams. Commonly, such a person is simply mistaken, doubtless influenced by a philistine view of dreams. I once came across a man who simply could not understand how an intellectual's description of experiences he had had of the fear of death could be genuine since his account was full of literary associations. He regarded these as retrospective additions. In his view, even an intellectual when confronted by extreme situations would inevitably abandon his superficial cultural gloss in favour of something more basic, the bare human necessities. He could not believe that reality and the way in which it is interpreted could be deeply affected by works of literature and that this symbiosis of reality and its literary interpretation constitutes the bare human necessities of the educated person.

Hence it simply will not do to inquire into the meaning of the triceratops that mysteriously make their appearance in Adorno's dreams without first pausing to ask why they are there in the first place. Nowadays, every child has a detailed knowledge of the different monsters that haunt Jurassic Park, and is at worst only ever in doubt about whether the pteranodons appeared in Part Three of that series or in Part Three of the Tolkien trilogy or whether they are really something from Harry Potter. In the 1950s the only people who could tell you about the names and characteristics of such creatures were people with a special interest. The Brockhaus encyclopaedia of 1957 has a brief entry for triceratops, but not for the ankylosaurus, which also appears in Adorno's dreams. The general interest in such creatures, and more especially the interest they had for Adorno, who anticipated their later popularity, is suggested by an article in Part One of *Minima Moralia* (which was completed in 1944). This book contains an entry entitled 'Mammoth', which describes the discovery of the skeleton of a dinosaur that had been reported in the American press 'some years previously'. His reflections on such discoveries are concerned with what he calls 'collective projections'[30] which may well precede their appearance in individualized dream images (especially since in both instances the triceratops resemble toys). It would be interesting to reflect on the degree to which such images had been determined by the way in which people had thought about them earlier – though perhaps this might be hard to decide.

On the other hand, these creatures act as bridging characters at an interesting emotional crossroads, one at which sexuality and death converge. The triceratops, for example, is one of those 'disgusting creatures' that 'create havoc'; elsewhere they are described as 'heads with tentacles', the source of an 'unspeakable horror' that lingers on into the waking state and which on one occasion, because the dream is enacted in Rome, Adorno surprisingly associates with the formation of a Maoist wing in the Italian Communist Party. In another dream, we see 'pretty children scrabbling around menacingly' and there is an 'indescribably horrifying dream' with 'monstrosities and extremely tiny dwarfs, including a bare negro head'; 'these monstrosities walked around on legs like lobsters, trying to attack people's genitals'. Whatever experiences were condensed into this fantasy, it is a highly oneiric motif, and it is situated at the precise point where temptation and fear are fused: 'I had the same fear', the dreamer notes, 'as a child has of a disreputable district or, later on, when a nightclub hostess grabbed me through my trousers.'

This anxiety dream is set in an establishment that the dreamer believes is a 'masochistic brothel',[31] which lacked, however, the freedom to come and go associated with such places: 'It sounded like mockery: we were all to be martyred.' Adorno's own MS notes contain a number of brothel dreams; 'Yet another brothel dream', he notes at one point. In *Minima Moralia*, he talks about 'the decline of the hotel', which is said to date back to 'the dissolution of the ancient unity of inn and brothel, nostalgia for which lives on in every glance directed at the displayed waitress and the tell-tale gestures of the chamber-maids.'[32] We may doubt the historical accuracy of this observation; its point is to make use of historical perspective so as to render visible the gap between reality and the image viewed with nostalgia. What counts here is our wish to be asked what we want. A number of the reflections in *Minima Moralia* are concerned with sexuality and love as wishes to be granted,[33] and the fact that mutuality in love does not operate on the principle of *do ut des* might well explain Adorno's excessive theoretical zeal to see the principle of exchange going everywhere about its destructive work when in reality connections are being established only by the overworked metaphor of equivalence. However that may be, his dream brothels are not sites of fulfilment. The dream-mother who is often present in them stands for both things: the principle of wish-fulfilment and of denial. In fact what happens mainly in these brothels is that people sit around, wear the wrong hats, an importunate waiter is resisted, the offer of a seminar on Heidegger is rejected amidst scenes of tumult, and a very beautiful naked girl 'has a flaw': 'she was made entirely of glass, or perhaps from the same elastic, transparent synthetic material that my new braces are made from.' The dreamer makes the age-old equation of intercourse and death, noting that 'intercourse [is] something I never dream of explicitly, any more than I dream of death.' Nevertheless, death is everywhere present, sometimes as an accident, but mainly in the shape of execution – his execution: 'I dreamed I was to be crucified' . . . 'The most agonizing method of execution – for which I was evidently destined' . . . 'Beheading'. . . 'Once again I was to be crucified.' Sometimes, it is the execution of someone else: 'Execution scene . . .' 'Execution of someone I knew . . .' and also 'execution under my command'. Lastly, there is the dream of a child handed over to the dream self for him to torture. There are both revulsion and attraction here. At issue is not death but torment. This theme emerged elsewhere too, in a noteworthy shift during Adorno's work on the *Lectures on Metaphysics* and its transformation into *Negative Dialectics*.[34] In the latter work, Adorno's ideas about the change in the meaning of death in the modern world are elucidated with reference to the way in which death had been turned into anonymous mass murder in the extermination camps and with reference also to the writings of Samuel Beckett (and this in turn stimulates him to attempt a reformulation of Western metaphysics). In the earlier book, in contrast, he had spoken of Jean-Paul Sartre's *Morts sans sépultures* [Men without Shadows] and Jean Amery's essay *On Torture* when he set out to describe the reality of the twentieth century, a reality that was supposed to enforce the paradoxical enterprise of a new grounding of metaphysics brought about by the historical experience of its impossibility. It is not the bureaucratic abolition of human beings but the traditional torment of the individual that gives Adorno his primary experience of terror. In the architecture of his intended theory that terror is once again rendered invisible and is supposed to be of no significance. We may read the *Dream Notes* as a protest against this erasure. There is a similar situation with regard to the remarks about Schoenberg's *A Survivor from Warsaw* (in 'Towards an Understanding of Schoenberg'), which are no doubt supposed to be admiring but which can scarcely conceal their ambivalence. The Frankfurt dream of July

1965 from which the dreamer awakens 'with a sense of horror' seems to call for a correction. At the same time, however, processions of the spirits of the dead drift through another dream in which we hear of 'Dreams of dead people in which you have the feeling that they are asking you for help.' Among these dreams is the one that is not included in the *Dream Notes*, but is mentioned in the *Lectures on Metaphysics* and *Negative Dialectics*, according to which 'he will be plagued by dreams that he is no longer living at all, that he was sent to the gas ovens in 1944 and his whole existence since has been imaginary'.[35] These dreams, then, are also the pre-reflexive cogito of a man who feels that both his thought and his existence, as well as the connection between the two, have become extremely fragile and questionable. His own image as a child emerges at one point as proof of his guilt, and it appears so insistently that the obvious comment that all guilt feelings represent simply the updating of childhood guilt feelings seems a little feeble, even though Adorno's use of the verses in Schubert's *Winterreise*: 'I have committed no crime – / Why should I flee mankind?' together with its slight misquotation,[36] precisely captures that element of the incomprehensible that accompanies childhood guilt feelings. In many people, he remarks in *Minima Moralia*, 'it is already an impertinence to say "I".'[37] But the I is perhaps always the mask one dons in order to be recognizable, to others and to oneself.

Night visions accompany the work. We can read the dream about Alban Berg's death as a part of the book about him, as something for which there was no space there, not even between the lines. At most, it could be added to the last sentence of the chapter entitled 'Reminiscences', which establishes such a powerful link between idealization and identification as already to enter into the intermediary realm of mourning and melancholy that the dreamer traverses.[38]

Examination panics. These too should be mentioned, even here. Freud had made the comforting observation that the exams we have nightmares about in our dreams are those that we have successfully passed in reality. Hence, such anxiety dreams really convey the encouraging assurance of the unconscious that we shall cope on this occasion as well. This may be so; I can scarcely believe it in the case of my own dreams, but let it pass. I would prefer to think about other aspects of the dream about the school essay on Goethe which Adorno dreamed on 4 September 1964 in Sils Maria. The task chosen by the dream self is an interpretation of Goethe's poem 'So let me seem till I become'. The dream self wishes to use this poem to explore 'the central complex' of Goethe's oeuvre, which he does in the following manner:

> My thesis went: Goethe endowed the language with so much earth that its gravity sank and released its content. I went to endless trouble to elaborate this idea. The mere writing down of each word cost me a huge effort and seemed to last an eternity. During this work I was in a panic about whether I could complete the task in the time available to me, and whether any teacher would be able to understand the essay . . .

In his essay on Goethe's *Elective Affinities* Adorno's friend Benjamin had compared the truth content of that work to the flame on a funeral pyre that rises above the coal and ashes that are left behind. Here, Adorno's dream reaches out to a gesture of burial: the heaped-up earth contains the remains that belong to it while the content is liberated and rises up. That is basically a reading of the poem itself, which is to be found in Book Eight of *Wilhelm Meister's Apprenticeship* and goes as follows:

> So let me seem till I become:
> Take not this garment white from me!
> I hasten from the joys of earth
> Down to that house so fast and firm.
>
> There will I rest in peace a while,
> Till opens wide my freshened glance.
> Then will I cast my dress aside,
> Leaving both wreath and girdle there.
>
> For all those glorious heavenly forms,
> They do not ask for man or wife,
> No garments long or draperies fine
> Surround the body now transformed.
>
> I lived indeed untouched by care.
> And yet I felt deep sorrow there,
> Sorrow has made me old too soon,
> Now make me young for ever more![39]

The fact that a person can choose such a poem, and that it can end like this, is somehow so self-explanatory that any dream narrative surrounding it is more or less reduced to the status of a stage direction and the accompanying feeling. 'I lived indeed untouched by care. / And yet I felt deep sorrow there': Adorno's memories of a childhood happiness with scarcely a shadow on it stand side by side with intimations of approaching evil, and his first experience of this, together with his visits to Germany from his exile in London, have something of the repetitive quality of dreams, as if he could see the evil but felt it could not touch him (although the letters in which he tells of his visits do not suggest he was under any illusions about conditions in Germany).

The Mignon motif, that in another place no questions are asked about man and woman, is presented in the poem as a heavenly promise, while in *Minima Moralia* Adorno speaks of an earth on which 'a limitless readiness to throw oneself away, which is as much beyond women in their fear as men in their arrogance',[40] cannot become anything more than a manner of speaking. And finally, the poem acts as a metaphor for Adorno's philosophy of art, which itself invokes the poem and perhaps dreams as witnesses: 'There is no work of art that does not promise that its truth content, to the extent that it appears in the work of art as something existing, realizes itself and leaves the work of art behind simply as a husk, as Mignon's prodigious verses prophesy.'[41]

We may add to this the 'central complex' of the author of these *Dream Notes*, namely the fear that, in the time allotted to him on earth, he might be unable to say all this in so compelling a fashion that it would be fully understood. His late essay 'Resignation'[42] seeks to shore up his confidence against this anxiety with the expressed hope that nothing that has once been thought through convincingly can be lost, because were that not so it would have to be thought anew. The idea of immortality, with which dreams are also concerned, is displaced here into the world of ideas. Behind this text stands death – Mignon cites Revelation 6: 9–15; the reader may wish to see for himself. The fact that ultimately the meanings that outgrow the works, as Mignon prophesies, amount to nothing, that Benjamin's metaphor of the flame ultimately vanishes, as Mephistopheles is aware while still in Arcadia, and that nothing remains but the realization that at best nothing remains but the pitiful mortal coil, has as much to do with the fear that is felt on awakening as with the end of *Negative Dialectics*, where Adorno declares his sense of solidarity with (traditional) metaphysics 'at the moment of its demise':

> Hang on to what, after all this, is left you!
> That dress – hold on to it! Already demons
> Eager to drag it to the underworld,
> Are snatching at its corners. Hang on tight!
> No longer your lost goddess, still it has
> Celestial attributes. Turn to account
> This priceless gift and soar on it aloft!
> As long as you endure it will transport you
> Through the skies, far from the common world.[43]

Perhaps *that* was the consolation, and the examination panic was ultimately consoling after all. The fact that the passage quoted goes on to promise post-mortal desolation is another story and is perhaps no more than wild surmise.

Jan Philipp Reemtsma

Notes

1 Ludwig Wittgenstein, *Last Writings on the Philosophy of Psychology*, trans. C. G. Luckhardt and Maximilian A. E. Aue, Oxford: Blackwell, 1982, vol. 1, p. 28e, no. 195 [Trans.].

2 Ludwig Wittgenstein, *Remarks on the Philosophy of Psychology*, trans. G. E. M. Anscombe, Oxford: Blackwell, 1980, vol. 1, p. 74e, no. 378.

3 See *Minima Moralia*, trans. Edmund Jephcott, London: NLB, 1974, p. 190.

4 Wieland Herzfelde, *Tragigrotesken der Nacht. Träume*, Berlin, 1920.

5 Ernst Jünger, *Träume*, in Jünger, *Sämtliche Werke*, vol. 13, Stuttgart, 1981, pp. 335–73.

6 Franz Fühmann, *Unter den Paranyas. Traum-Erzählungen und – Notate*, in Fühmann, *Werke*, vol. 7, Rostock, 1993, pp. 207–388.

7 Ibid., p. 231.

8 In Fühmann's case, we can sometimes make the comparison. If you take as an example the 'Traum von der Steppe' [Dream of the Steppes], the 1973 version begins, 'I am standing in a steppe of silent, sad, rainy grey which merges in each of its lines with the silent, grey sky' (p. 269). Ten years later, he writes: 'I am standing in a steppe of silent grey, that merges in each of its faded lines with the silent, grey sky' (p. 232). Similarly, the end of the 1973 version went: 'Blow, blow, I think and pass away imperceptibly into the grey void.' In the later version, this becomes: 'Blow, blow, I think and pass away enraptured into the grey universe.'

9 Walter Benjamin, *One-Way Street*, in *Selected Writings*, vol. 1: *1913–1926*, ed. Marcus Bullock and Michael W. Jennings, trans. Edmund Jephcott, Cambridge, MA, and London: Belknap Press of Harvard University Press, 1996, 'Breakfast Room', p. 444f.

10 Ibid., p. 445.

11 Ibid., 'Cellar' and 'Dining Hall', p. 445.

12 Friedrich de la Motte Fouqué (1777–1843) was a prolific and widely read author of Romantic stories and novels. His best known tale is 'Undine', a story about a mermaid, which has come to symbolize Romanticism [Trans.].

Afterword

13 Walter Benjamin, *Selected Writings*, vol. 1, 'Vestibule', p. 445.
14 Ibid., vol. 2, 'Surrealism', p. 208.
15 Ibid., 'Dream Kitsch', p. 4.
16 Theodor W. Adorno, 'Looking Back on Surrealism', in *Notes to Literature*, trans. Shierry Weber Nicholsen, New York: Columbia University Press, 1991, vol. 1, p. 87.
17 This is another way of agreeing with Freud's remark that the assertion that dreams are wish-fulfilments and the assertion that dreams are the attempt at a wish-fulfilment make the same statement.
18 With regard to the following comments, see Jan Philipp Reemtsma, 'Der Traum von der Ich-Ferne. Adornos literarische Aufsätze', a lecture given on 25 September 2003 at the Adorno Conference held at the Institute of Social Research in Frankfurt and published in *Mittelweg 36: Zeitschrift des Hamburger Instituts für Sozialforschung*, no. 6, 2003, pp. 3–40.
19 Theodor W. Adorno, *Aesthetic Theory*, trans. Robert Hullot-Kentor, New York: Continuum, 2002, p. 93.
20 Theodor W. Adorno, 'On the Classicism of Goethe's *Iphigenie*', in *Notes to Literature*, vol. 2, p. 155.
21 *Aesthetic Theory*, p. 322.
22 *Minima Moralia*, p. 192.
23 *Aesthetic Theory*, p. 74.
24 *Minima Moralia*, p. 170.
25 Quoted from Jan Philipp Reemtsma, 'Der Traum von der Ich-Ferne', p. 38f.
26 Theodor W. Adorno, *Vorlesung über Negative Dialektik*, ed. Rolf Tiedemann, Frankfurt am Main: Suhrkamp, 2003, p. 104.
27 Interestingly, shamanism is readily accepted by people who regard psychoanalysis as hocus-pocus.
28 'Little Nemo' is the main fictional character in a series of weekly comic strips by Winsor McCay (1887–1934) that appeared in the *New York Herald* and William Randolph Hearst's *New York American* between 1905 and 1913 [Trans.].

29 'Magd' = maid or virgin [Trans.].

30 *Minima Moralia*, p. 115f.

31 Not: 'a Maoist brothel', in which crèpe de chine and tarty [*halb-seiden*] go together.

32 *Minima Moralia*, p. 117.

33 For example, 'Inter pares', p. 32, 'May I be so bold?', p. 90, 'The truth about Hedda Gabler', p. 93, and 'Since I set eyes on him', p. 95.

34 On what follows, see Jan Philipp Reemtsma, ' "Ja, wenn der Beckett im Konzentrationslager gewesen wäre . . ." Überlegungen anläßlich einer in der *Negativen Dialektik* mitgeteilten Anekdote', in Reemtsma, *Warum Hagen den Ortlieb erschlug. Unzeitgemäßes über Krieg und Tod*, Munich, 2003, pp. 250–66.

35 *Negative Dialectics*, trans. E. B. Ashton, London: Routledge, 1996, p. 363.

36 Adorno's use of 'flee' [*fliehn*] replaced the 'shun' [*scheun*] of Wilhelm Müller's original text [Trans.].

37 *Minima Moralia*, p. 50.

38 The last sentence of 'Reminiscences' reads: 'He successfully avoided becoming an adult without remaining infantile.' *Alban Berg: Master of the Smallest Link*, trans. Juliane Brand and Christopher Hailey, Cambridge: Cambridge University Press, 1991, p. 34 [Trans.].

39 Johann Wolfgang von Goethe, *William Meister's Apprenticeship*, ed. and trans. E. A. Blackall in cooperation with Victor Lange, in Goethe, *The Collected Works*, Princeton, NJ: Princeton University Press, 1995, vol. 9, p. 316.

40 *Minima Moralia*, p. 91.

41 *Aesthetic Theory*, p. 132.

42 See 'Resignation', in *Critical Models*, trans. Henry Pickford, New York: Columbia University Press, 1998, pp. 289–95.

43 Johann Wolfgang von Goethe, *Faust*, Part Two, trans. Stuart Atkins, in Goethe, *The Collected Works*, Princeton, NJ: Princeton University Press, 1994, vol. 2, p. 250f.

— Index —